GEORGIANA AND KITTY CHRISTMAS AT PEMBERLEY

BY LAUREN GUNDERSON AND MARGOT MELCON

DRAMATISTS PLAY SERVICE

GEORGIANA AND KITTY: CHRISTMAS AT PEMBERLEY was commissioned and originally produced by the Jungle Theater (Christina Baldwin, Artistic Director; Robin Gillette, Managing Director), Minneapolis, Minnesota; Marin Theatre Company (Jasson Minadakis, Artistic Director; Meredith Suttles, Managing Director), Mill Valley, California; and Northlight Theatre (BJ Jones, Artistic Director; Timothy J. Evans, Executive Director), Skokie, Illinois, in 2021 and 2022.

At the Jungle Theater, it was directed by Christina Baldwin and Angela Timberman, the scenic and costume designs were by Sarah Bahr, the lighting design was by Marcus Dilliard, the sound design was by C Andrew Mayer, the music arranger and violinist was Emilia Mettenbrink, and the properties designer and stage manager was John Novak. The cast was as follows:

GEORGIANA DARCY	Marisa B. Tejeda
KITTY BENNET	Becca Hart
ELIZABETH DARCY	Sun Mee Chomet
LYDIA WICKHAM	Adelin Phelps
JANE BINGLEY	Maggie Cramer
MARY BENNET	Vinecia Coleman
HENRY GREY	Dustin Bronson
THOMAS O'BRIEN	Tom Reed
FITZWILLIAM DARCY	James Rodríguez

At the Marin Theatre Company, it was directed by Meredith Mc-Donough, the scenic design was by Nina Ball, the costume design was by Fumiko Bielefeldt, the lighting design was by Wen-Ling Liao, the sound design was by Madeleine Oldham, the composition and musical direction was by Jenny Giering, and the stage manager was Elisa Guthertz. The cast was as follows:

GEORGIANA DARCY	Lauren Spencer
KITTY BENNET	Emilie Whelan
ELIZABETH DARCY	Laura Odeh
LYDIA WICKHAM/SARAH DARCY	Madeline Rouverol
JANE BINGLEY/EMILY GREY	Aidaa Peerzada

MARY BENNET/MARGARET O'BRIEN .... Alicia M. P. Nelson
HENRY GREY .... Zahan F. Mehta
THOMAS O'BRIEN .... Adam Magill
FITZWILLIAM DARCY .... Daniel Duque-Estrada

At the Northlight Theatre, it was directed by Marti Lyons, the set design was by Richard and Jacqueline Penrod, the lighting design was by Jason Lynch, the costume design was by Raquel Adorno, and the original music and sound design were by Christopher Kriz. The cast was as follows:

GEORGIANA DARCY .... Janyce Caraballo
KITTY BENNET .... Samantha Newcomb
ELIZABETH DARCY .... Amanda Drinkall
LYDIA WICKHAM .... Preeti Thaker
JANE BINGLEY .... Emma Jo Boyden
MARY BENNET .... Andrea San Miguel
HENRY GREY .... Erik Hellman
THOMAS O'BRIEN .... Nate Santana
FITZWILLIAM DARCY .... Yousof Sultani

CHARACTERS

Act One—1815, Christmas, Pemberley

GEORGIANA DARCY—Mr. Darcy's younger sister, shy, an accomplished pianist, romantic though super hesitant after her experience with Wickham. She is an introvert but lives a full life in the letters she writes and the music she plays. Very like her brother in some ways, she can be stubborn and a bit of a grudge holder.

KITTY BENNET—second-to-youngest Bennet sister, a ray of sunshine, the perfect best friend and wingman, she is supportive, optimistic, and a problem solver. Without the influence of Lydia, she is now more grounded and generous. She is the mastermind behind Georgiana's future.

ELIZABETH DARCY—second-to-eldest Bennet sister, married to Mr. Darcy, bright and witty, she loves all of her sisters but loves Georgiana as both a sister and a mother figure, and brings Georgiana out in a way that Darcy tends to shut her down.

LYDIA WICKHAM—youngest Bennet sister, a little extra but has gained some wisdom. Now that she is suddenly without a husband she is looking for a companion again, only to find Kitty unavailable.

JANE BINGLEY—eldest and most reserved sister of the Bennets. Married to Bingley and very pregnant with her first child. Kind, generous, soft-spoken.

MARY BENNET—middle sister, brainy, sharp-tongued, and extremely recently engaged to Arthur de Bourgh.

HENRY GREY—Georgiana's beau—also remarkably shy and an introvert, but of incredible sincerity and intellect. Henry is unassuming, possibly to a fault, and is unaware that he is the hero of the story.

THOMAS O'BRIEN—Henry's friend, a little bawdy and a little jolly, says exactly what's on his mind, does not have much time for polite society but is so good-natured that everyone just kind of loves him.

FITZWILLIAM DARCY—proud and still finding his warmth, does not forgive easily, perhaps slightly overprotective of his little sister.

Act Two—Six years later, 1821, Christmas, London

Same characters, a little older, a little wiser.

GEORGIANA AND KITTY CHRISTMAS AT PEMBERLEY

ACT ONE

Prologue

We see Georgiana reading a series of letters, from Lizzy, Kitty, Henry, and Darcy. As they are read, she becomes increasingly overwhelmed.

KITTY. Dearest Georgie,
How I have missed you since I left London and returned to Long-bourn. It is not nearly so much fun here, without the pleasures of society and most especially without the joy of seeing you, my very best friend. I shall join you soon at Pemberley on Christmas morning and I. Cannot. Wait! Of course you will have to anchor yourself in the very wild sea of Bennets, but you shall always have me as a safe harbor. Your dear friend, Kitty Bennet

LIZZY. Darling Georgiana,
How impatiently Mr. Darcy and I await your arrival to Pemberley for the holiday! Though he will not admit it, your brother misses you terribly since you have been so much in London. He believes you prefer concertos to his company, and I haven't the heart to tell him that he is probably correct. With great anticipation of your arrival home, Lizzy

DARCY. Sister,
Your correspondence in the last weeks has become sparse, which can hopefully be credited to a dedication to and advancement of your intellectual pursuits. I do look forward to hearing details of your activities and acquaintances. I welcome your return for

Christmas, we Darcys are outnumbered by Bennets threefold. Come quickly. Your brother, Fitzwilliam Darcy

HENRY. Dear Miss Darcy,

Your last letter has given me so much to consider, with mentions of Mozart, thoughts on intervals that have confounded and inspired me, and the very humorous story about your attempt to play *Moonlight* Sonata backward! But my sole purpose in writing today is to accept your generous offer to visit Pemberley. If you are certain it would not be an imposition, I can think of nothing more delightful than to see you in person after our long correspondence. Humbly, Mr. Henry Grey

GEORGIANA. *(Joyful!)* He's coming! *(Suddenly terribly anxious.)* He's coming.

  Transition to…

Scene 1

Pemberley Estate, late Christmas morning.

The drawing room is full and bustling with chatter and excitement.

Presents are given and opened and complimented.

A peacock-feather pen from Darcy to Lizzy.
A lace shawl for Jane from Lizzy.
Piano sheet music for Georgiana from Darcy.
A small painting of Pemberley by Lizzy for Darcy.
Books, books, books for Mary.
Ribbons, ribbons, ribbons for Lydia.
An embroidered handkerchief from Georgiana to Darcy.
Blank sheet music from Kitty to Georgiana.

Lizzy, Lydia, Jane, Mary, Kitty talk all at once.

LIZZY.	JANE.	MARY.
How wonderful!	I love it, Lizzy!	Whoever gave this to me thank you!

KITTY.	LYDIA.
Happy Christmas!	Yes Yes Yes! What did I get?

LIZZY. It's magnificent, darling! My correspondence will suddenly have so much more character!

KITTY. Look at that!

MARY. Is that a peacock feather?

DARCY. I thought it suited you.

MARY. A lovely specimen.

LIZZY. I adore it!

LYDIA. Is that for your hair?

LIZZY. No, it is for writing.

LYDIA. What a shame to waste it on *that*.

JANE. *Lydia.*

LYDIA. If I were a peacock I should be furious.

KITTY. You and peacocks would certainly have a lot to talk about.

      Mary cackles at this.

LIZZY. Would you two stop pecking at each other?

JANE. I do love this shawl, Lizzy. And it's one of the few garments I can still manage to wear.

LYDIA. The lace is exquisite.   **KITTY.** Gorgeous!

LIZZY. You deserve something as beautiful as you.

JANE. Oh stop. What did you get, Mary?

MARY. *(Revealing a small tower of books she got as gifts.)* Books. From every single person I know. And I thank you all.

KITTY. Those should keep you busy for a day or two.

DARCY. Did I choose the right composer, Georgiana? I requested what I thought would be the most enjoyable and challenging music for you.

GEORGIANA. Mozart is perfect. Thank you so much.

MARY. Oooh Mozart? May I see?

KITTY. Oh, Georgie! I got you something similar but all your own! Open it, open it!

GEORGIANA. You shouldn't have, Kitty.

LYDIA. Georgiana gets a present from Kitty, but I don't?

KITTY. I got you ribbons, Lydia!

LYDIA. That is what you always get me. That is all anyone ever gets me.

GEORGIANA. Oh, how thoughtful!

LIZZY. What is it?

KITTY. It's music. Or it will be.

MARY. It's blank!

KITTY. Yes, because Georgiana will write her *own*.

LIZZY. What   **JANE.** How interesting!   **LYDIA.** What for?
a perfect idea!

MARY. May I have the Mozart then?

DARCY. It does seem quite uncommon.

GEORGIANA. Oh, I only dally with my own music, I could never compose.

KITTY. You must or that poor paper shall remain forever bare. (*Making the sheet music "talk."*) "Don't abandon me, Georgiana!"

> *Kitty and Georgiana giggle like very best friends, Lydia notices.*

LYDIA. When did they become such friends?

MARY. When you moved away, and she moved on.

> *A side conversation between Lizzy and Darcy.*

DARCY. How was I to know that she wanted *blank* sheet music?

LIZZY. It sounds like *she* didn't know she wanted blank sheet music. Darling, your gift is lovely. And if you do not know what a young lady likes, that is only because you, my dear, are not a young lady.

DARCY. I most certainly am not.

LIZZY. Though now I am imagining you with ribbons and needle-work!

DARCY. Would you please desist so that I might maintain a shred of dignity in my own home.

LIZZY. Then occupy me, lest I say too much.

> *With a kiss, he does.*

MARY. There is far too much happening in the corner, Lizzy. There are unmarried ladies present.

KITTY. Unmarried only for now, Mary!

MARY. That is accurate and still remarkable.

LYDIA. I remain thoroughly shocked.

JANE. No, Mary's engagement to Mr. de Bourgh is just as it should be.

DARCY. A surprise certainly, but what a fine one.

LIZZY. We are overjoyed for you darling!

GEORGIANA. Such wonderful—

LYDIA. (*Interrupting.*) Does no one else find it absolutely preposterous that Lizzy no longer has the most successful match among us *because of Mary*?!

JANE. Oh **LIZZY.** Lydia. **KITTY.** Oh **MARY.** Thank you
Lydia, stop. please. for your support.

MARY. Earlier this morning you seemed almost pleased for me,
Lydia, and now you have returned to the Lydia we all know and…
well, the Lydia we all know.

KITTY. Let her be, Lydia.

LYDIA. Oh, don't worry, Kitty, you'll marry soon, and you know
no one expects much from the last of five sisters.

KITTY. In that case I shall renounce marriage entirely and spend all
my time having terrifically interesting conversations with Georgiana.

LYDIA. How ever can you tell she is interesting when she barely
says a word!

GEORGIANA. Actually, I—

JANE. It is possible that she simply cannot be heard among the five
of us and our bickering.

GEORGIANA. I'm sure I could—

LIZZY. It isn't as though she never speaks, she is simply thoughtful
and reserved.

GEORGIANA. Of course, I—

DARCY. *(Interrupting.)* If I may say, Darcys have always been
known to choose our words carefully.

> *A pause, as they all look to Georgiana to finally speak and
> all she says is—*

GEORGIANA. Indeed.

JANE. I believe I'll return upstairs to rest before Christmas dinner,
though it may take me a moment and some effort. Lydia, will you
join me?

LYDIA. Why must I?

JANE. To help me and distract you.

LIZZY. I'll come, Jane dear.

JANE. Bring biscuits.

LIZZY. Of course. **LYDIA.** With the orangey bits!

LYDIA. *(Calling to Kitty, expecting her to follow like she used to.)* Come along, Kitty, we shall entertain ourselves.

KITTY. I am perfectly happy with Georgiana. Go with Jane.

LYDIA. I don't want to go with Jane.

KITTY. And I needn't be bothered with your every decision, have a lovely afternoon.

LYDIA. Kitty!

 JANE. Lydia!

  LIZZY. Biscuits!

DARCY. I believe I shall consult with Mrs. Reynolds about the gifts for the household staff.

MARY. And I'll go find Mr. de Bourgh and show him my new books. *Our* books. This constant state of smiling is exhausting.

> *Mary is off to find Mr. de Bourgh; Lydia and Lizzy help Jane offstage; Darcy disappears downstairs. Kitty and Georgiana are left alone. Georgiana is a different person when she is alone with Kitty—at ease.*

KITTY. *(Laughing and collapsing into the nearest chair.)* Oh, how I have NOT missed this fussing about. I do love them, but they are impossible.

GEORGIANA. And yet you are able to speak and laugh and join in as much as the rest of them. How ever do you manage it?

KITTY. Years of practice. You seem to be the only one who is never allowed a single word!

GEORGIANA. I am used to it. Years of practice.

KITTY. I am sorry about Lydia. I never used to see the harm, but now her inconsiderate prattling feels more intentional than it once did.

GEORGIANA. Lydia does not mean harm.

KITTY. Doesn't she? As a girl I used to follow her every impulse like a duckling tripping after its mother. But now all I see is her vanity and selfishness. Even now! Here I am talking about *her* when we could be planning all manner of merriment for ourselves.

GEORGIANA. I am so pleased your sister married my brother.

KITTY. It was thoughtful of them. What would I do without you?

GEORGIANA. You would be fabulously bored I imagine. Did you open my gift? I do hope you like it.

KITTY. I will adore it because you gave it to me. *(Opening it, gasping at the lilac stationery set of fine paper.)* Oh, but I actually *do* adore it! My own stationery! Oh, it's marvelous! And my favorite color!

GEORGIANA. I'm so glad you will enjoy it.

KITTY. I will! And because you are my most frequent correspondent, *you* will likewise enjoy it!

GEORGIANA. I might have bought some for myself in blue. It was simply too beautiful.

KITTY. Then will Mr. Henry Grey also enjoy it?

GEORGIANA. Oh stop, please stop. I'm already bursting with nerves about him.

KITTY. Has he written again?

GEORGIANA. He writes daily.

KITTY. Because he admires you.

GEORGIANA. Because he enjoys music!

KITTY. Because he employs music as a means to be closer to you.

GEORGIANA. Please stop! I am much more comfortable discussing harmonic progressions than Mr. Grey's affections.

KITTY. I am less interested in his affections, and more so in yours. Do you love him?

GEORGIANA. Even if I do—or might—or think I might—when I was in love before, it was not like this.

KITTY. What you felt for Mr. Wickham was not love.

GEORGIANA. But at the time I thought it was. This is my concern. I cannot trust myself to know what I feel.

KITTY. Yes, you can. That is what experience teaches us. Your encounter with Wickham taught you to discern a scoundrel, and Henry is no such thing. What did your brother say when you told him of your correspondence?

GEORGIANA. My brother…does not yet know.

KITTY. What? Georgiana, we agreed! Why didn't you tell him? We must remedy this if it is to proceed. At least Lizzy knows.

GEORGIANA. Lizzy knows? Did you tell her?

KITTY. No, I did not tell Lizzy. *You* were going to tell her. You didn't tell Lizzy either?!

GEORGIANA. No! I cannot think of what to say, not to Lizzy and especially not to my brother. He does not trust men, or does not trust me, or does not trust men near me.

KITTY. Mr. Darcy will release that judgment. But you must be honest with him.

GEORGIANA. And I wish to be honest, but I also wish to protect what Henry and I have. *(A breath.)* Though we said no more than a few words to each other after that concert, when we started a correspondence it was as though I was writing to a friend I'd always known. I thought if I spoke of this perfect intimacy to anyone but you, it would vanish.

KITTY. It will not vanish if it's real. You must give him the opportunity to know you, and you him, outside of letters. But if your brother is not informed at once, this friendship you have been forming will have been for naught. Perhaps if you invite Mr. Grey to call some time in the new year...?

> *Beat. Confession.*

GEORGIANA. He is coming. Tomorrow. Mr. Grey is coming tomorrow.

KITTY. Coming?

> **GEORGIANA.** To Pemberley.

> > **KITTY.** *Tomorrow? To Pemberley?!*

GEORGIANA. Yes and he's bringing a friend and they are making their way through this part of the country and I thought what a fine time to ask him to call and, I don't know, sing a carol and have some tea and, oh dear god what have I done.

KITTY. *Georgiana, at Christmas!* In the midst of your entire family?! *And mine!*

GEORGIANA. It was only just settled in the days before I left London and I didn't tell my brother before because I thought it better to tell him in person and then I didn't and now it is too late, so, I just…won't.

KITTY. *(Laughing.)* Well, Mr. Grey is very quiet, perhaps Mr. Darcy will not notice he is here at all.

GEORGIANA. You will not joke about this, Kitty!

KITTY. Do not get angry with *me*, this is entirely your doing! At the very least we must tell Lizzy you are expecting a guest.

GEORGIANA. Two.

KITTY. *Two. Yes. GO. NOW.*

GEORGIANA. *YesYesYes, all right, I am going.*

> *Kitty forces Georgiana to find Lizzy.*

Scene 2

Lizzy and Darcy, later on Christmas Day.

DARCY. SHE WHAT. WHAT DID SHE SAY TO YOU?

LIZZY. She said they met at a salon in London in January, and they have been corresponding since.

DARCY. January?! Nearly a year of letters she has been writing and receiving and she never mentioned it? Not to you, nor to me?

LIZZY. She told Kitty. Kitty says he is quite nice.

DARCY. Oh, well, lovely. If Kitty says he is quite nice, then my mind is utterly liberated. This is why I resisted her playing at these salons.

LIZZY. Oh but they're so popular in London. So many artists and writers and intellectuals. It sounds perfectly divine.

DARCY. It sounds improper for a young lady to play in public unaccompanied.

LIZZY. Oh, I'm sure there was a violinist. *(Cracking herself up.)* I'm sorry, so sorry.

DARCY. Lizzy, my god. This is the reputation of my one and only sister, whose life is mine to secure and protect.

LIZZY. And hers to live! I understand why she did not want to tell you, though I am disappointed that she did not tell me.

> *A questioning look from Darcy.*

I do not know if you are aware, darling, but you can be difficult to speak to.

DARCY. I have no idea what you mean.

LIZZY. You can be a dreadful and stubborn goose! You judge prematurely, decline to change your opinion, and you guard your sister to a fault.

DARCY. I have many extraordinary reasons to guard her.

LIZZY. They have been corresponding about music. There is nothing objectionable in that.

DARCY. I object to the fact that she concealed this from me. This has happened once before with Wickham and without my involvement he would have ruined her.

LIZZY. Instead he lured away Lydia and ruined *her.*

DARCY. Which is why I put the man in his place.

LIZZY. With your fist, and bravo.

DARCY. Thank you, it was very satisfying.

LIZZY. What happened to Georgiana was Wickham's moral failure, not hers. She was so young when he convinced her to elope. She is certainly more self-aware now than she was at fifteen. Allow her to show us who she *is,* not forever hold her to her past.

DARCY. I have for so long been the only one protecting her. Since our parents passed, I have been more father than brother to her. Wickham's plot exposed my failings as both. I will welcome Mr. Grey into our home, but not without inquiry. I do not trust him.

LIZZY. You do not know him!

DARCY. Precisely.

LIZZY. He is not Wickham, dear.

DARCY. Good, if he has nothing to conceal he will not object to interrogation—

LIZZY. You will lose her.

> *This stops Darcy cold.*

You will lose her if you cage her. If you deny her choice in love and life, she will turn from you. Your expectations of perfection and hasty judgment almost lost us our life together. Do not let the same prejudices drive your only sister from you.

DARCY. What if this man exposes her to disappointment and heartbreak?

LIZZY. That is what it is to be alive. You cannot protect her from living.

DARCY. Perhaps you are…right.

LIZZY. Perhaps I am. Now, may we resume some semblance of Christmas festivities or would you prefer to grumble in the corner.

DARCY. I'll thank you not to mock me when it comes to my sister.

LIZZY. I love you, darling, but if we cannot mock one another now and then it will be a long life indeed.

> *She starts to exit but Mr. Darcy does a fine Mr. Darcy move and grabs her hand, pulls his wife back into the kiss we all want. They exit.*

Scene 3

> *Morning, Boxing Day. Kitty and Georgiana enter, relieved and conspiring.*

KITTY. I have truly never been more excited for a Boxing Day in my life. Do you know when they mean to arrive?

GEORGIANA. I know nothing. Which combined with the fact that I could not sleep last night makes me both anxious and unprepared. As though someone has handed me an instrument and told me to play a brand new concerto.

KITTY. Honestly, you could probably manage that.

GEORGIANA. It depends on the instrument!

KITTY. Do not worry, Lizzy will help Mr. Darcy understand. And I will not leave your side.

> *Lydia enters, looking for someone to talk to.*

LYDIA. Lord, Kitty, how I long for this holiday to end. I am exhausted and so much has happened it is not to be believed!

GEORGIANA. Hello, Lydia.

LYDIA. Oh. *You're* here. Huzzah.

KITTY. Georgiana and I were in the middle of a conversation, Lydia.

LYDIA. Well, it cannot be nearly as important as what has just happened to me! I have done something completely shocking and you will be most proud of me. Did you know Mr. Wickham was here, downstairs, at Pemberley?

GEORGIANA. *What?!*

KITTY. *Lydia, do not mention that man!*

LYDIA. Why not, he's gone now, because I just sent him away myself, thank you very much.

GEORGIANA. He was here?

LYDIA. He certainly was! To whisk me away and beg my forgiveness, but I told him I will no longer be his pet, my life is my own, and he shall remain out of it! Today is a new day!

KITTY. Which is very good for you and not of concern for us. There is more at hand than another disagreement between you and your husband.

LYDIA. This is not "another disagreement," Wickham is gone *for good*! At minimum I expect you to notice.

KITTY. You expect me to provide you with undivided attention. I'm sorry Lydia. I am very glad that you have freed yourself from that man. But every letter you have written in the past two years has been about how grand *your* life is, the fun *you* have, the parties *you* attend. And now, still, all you can think of is the latest affair unfolding in *your* life instead of how that news might affect others.

In two years of letters, you have not asked a single thing about me. Two years! In that same time, I have met uncommonly curious and bright people, people like Georgiana, who talk to me and are interested in what I have to say and who care about me beyond my ability to provide them an audience. We are all relieved that your husband has departed and that we are spared his company. But do not turn to me, demanding I listen, now that *you* are unoccupied.

Lydia is stung by this.

GEORGIANA. Lydia…

LYDIA. No, I… I…

> *Lydia is terribly embarrassed, hurt, and angry. She storms out of the room.*

KITTY. I am so sorry.

GEORGIANA. I cannot believe he was here.

KITTY. Your brother was never going to let him near you, I'm quite sure of that. I am only sorry Lydia felt the need to reveal his presence at all.

GEORGIANA. No, no. I do not resent her. Wickham tricked her as much as he did me. I am glad for her and her…freedom.

KITTY. How can you stand to be so *kind. Ugh.* I suppose I should apologize to her. Lydia just infuriates me with her self-importance. She always intrudes! On everything!

GEORGIANA. She is envious of you.

KITTY. Of me? No one is envious of me.

GEORGIANA. Of course they are! You are clever and kind and so much fun. You have such an effortless way about you.

KITTY. Really? Thank you. With a house full of sisters such as mine, I was always just…around. Then, as everyone left home suddenly there was so much room for me to be. I rather like being me, as it turns out.

GEORGIANA. I like it too. You make an art of caring for others. And now, you must engage your charms and ensure I do not behave foolishly when Mr. Grey arrives today.

KITTY. You should simply speak with the same confidence with which you write.

GEORGIANA. If only it were so simple as that.

> *Jane, Mary, Lizzy, and Darcy enter, giddy and thrilled as Lizzy and Darcy have just told everyone that they are pregnant.*

MARY. Oh it's just the most wonderful news Lizzy!

JANE. I knew it would happen soon, I just knew.

KITTY. What's all this?

MARY. Lizzy is expecting! They just told us!

LIZZY. By accident.

DARCY. It flew out, I do apologize.

> *Kitty hugs Lizzy.*

KITTY. Oh Lizzy! My goodness, all of this joy in one holiday!

GEORGIANA. Brother! What news!

> *Georgiana goes to Darcy to hug him. For Darcy there is more in this hug than congratulations. He wants to tell her more.*

MARY. How perfect that you and Jane will have children so near the same age.

JANE. They'll be inseparable.

LIZZY. Just as we were as girls.

GEORGIANA. I could not be happier, brother.

DARCY. Thank you. You will make the perfect aunt.

LIZZY. And piano tutor.

KITTY. Well, I plan on making messes with this little girl as often as I am allowed.

LIZZY. A little girl?!

DARCY. We cannot know anything of the sort.

KITTY. But of course, it will be a girl.

MARY. It is absolutely going to be a girl.

JANE. How wonderful! A girl!

GEORGIANA. Imagine, a little baby Lizzy!

DARCY. *(Imagining two strong-willed women in his house making trouble.)* For that, I am not convinced that I, nor the world, is fully prepared.

LIZZY. Leave this wonderful man in peace. Now, all we need is a name for the baby and all will be resolved!

JANE. Well, take care who you bring into that particular discussion. I have been drowned by suggestions from Mr. Bingley's sister since we first revealed we were in a family way. She was displeased with every consideration, to the point where I finally conceded that the only obvious choice was to name the baby Caroline after her, just to end the conversation.

KITTY. And if it is a boy?

JANE. Caroline either way if I am to have any peace.

LIZZY. I love it!

MARY. Mr. Darcy, aren't you relieved the family you married into is refreshingly free from opinion?

Darcy laughs at that idea.

LIZZY. *(Saving him.)* Darling, should you not go find Mr. Bingley and Mr. de Bourgh?

DARCY. Yes…and any remaining brandy. A word, Georgiana?

GEORGIANA. Of course, brother.

They move to the side. Lizzy moves to join them but Darcy waves her away.

DARCY. I am fully aware that Mrs. Darcy is orchestrating my exit so I shall not be present for the arrival of your visitors.

GEORGIANA. I am sorry I have not been as truthful as I should have.

DARCY. I do not wish to be the kind of brother you cannot confide in. I remain open to receiving your guests, but you must be open with me. That is the only way I will be able to fulfill my most important duty of being your guardian. My only wish is for your happiness.

Georgiana really needed to hear that.

GEORGIANA. I know. I do.

DARCY. And I would like to know about the gentleman. Tell me why he has…caught your attention?

GEORGIANA. Oh brother, he is intelligent and kind and eloquent— especially when we write of music. He is quite perfect I think.

DARCY. And what of his family?

GEORGIANA. The Greys are a very good family by all accounts, with an estate in Chester and both brothers attending Oxford like their father did before them. I do not think there is an objection to be found.

DARCY. MmHmm.

LIZZY. If Georgiana has no objection, I cannot imagine we will find fault.

DARCY. I look forward to welcoming him.

Georgiana hugs him so hard.

GEORGIANA. Thank you! And I know you will welcome him with perfect kindness.

DARCY. I shall.
Try.

GEORGIANA. Brother!   **LIZZY.** Mr. Darcy do not tease the poor girl.

DARCY. *(Departing.)* I will be on my best behavior. Sister. Ladies.

JANE. Good day, Mr. Darcy.   **LIZZY.** Enjoy, darling.

Darcy kisses Lizzy and exits. Georgiana is suddenly anxious.

MARY. What did I hear? What gentlemen are arriving, Lizzy?

KITTY and LIZZY. Georgiana's friends.

GEORGIANA. Acquaintance is more accurate.

LIZZY. You assured me that you knew him, I convinced your brother that he was respectable!

GEORGIANA. He is! In letters.

MARY. You've never met him?!

KITTY. No! Of course she has met him…once.

LIZZY. Once?!

JANE. Just the once?

LIZZY. And you invited him at Christmas.

GEORGIANA. I invited him at Christmas. This is absurd, you are very right. We should stop the whole thing. Tell Mrs. Reynolds that when they arrive she must turn them away!

KITTY. Georgie,   **JANE.** No, you   **LIZZY.** Don't be
no!   mustn't!   silly.

GEORGIANA. But I fear I will have nothing to say and he will regret calling but then he will be forced to stay and I will be miserable and he will be miserable and I shall never get to play him the Mozart

I've practiced! And that is to say nothing of how my brother will behave toward him!

MARY. That is more words in one speech than I have heard you say in our entire acquaintance.

LIZZY. They've come all this way.

KITTY. And they're not an invading army.

JANE. It is going to be just fine, Georgiana. Mr. Darcy loves you and will welcome Mr. Grey because he is a gentleman and he knows his position dictates civility, at the very least.

LIZZY. That's the spirit.

MARY. Or the hope.

GEORGIANA. But what if it goes terribly wrong?

MARY. Distract them with music.

KITTY. Yes, Mr. Grey loves your playing as much as Mr. Darcy does.

LIZZY. Perfect! Unite them in praise of you.

GEORGIANA. I don't want praise, I want to run away to the attic.

KITTY. You are going to have to suffer through some compliments so you ought to steady yourself.

MARY. Or perhaps Mr. Darcy would share some of that brandy?

JANE. Mary, that's ridiculous!   **KITTY.** I wouldn't say no.   **MARY.** For nerves.

Before Georgiana can respond, Lydia walks in.

LYDIA. A carriage has just arrived. Are we expecting anyone?

KITTY. They're here!   **JANE.** Oh, my word.   **MARY.** And we're off.   **LIZZY.** Oh goodness it's happening.

GEORGIANA. No no no no.

LYDIA. Who is here?

KITTY, MARY, and LIZZY. GENTLEMEN.

LYDIA. WHAT KIND?!

GEORGIANA. We should have kept this all on paper.

KITTY. But the way he wrote of wanting to hear you play again in his letters!

GEORGIANA. *You cannot mention that I let you read his letters!*

KITTY. I would never, of course I would never!

MARY. I want to read his letters.

LYDIA. Me too!

KITTY, JANE, and LIZZY. NO LETTERS.

MARY. I hear the door.

KITTY. They're being shown down the hall.

GEORGIANA. I'm going to faint.

JANE. Sit down!

LIZZY. Can we please try to appear as though we are sensible!

MARY. Oh, I believe that moment has passed.

THOMAS. *(Offstage.)* Good afternoon?

> *They all freeze. The door opens. Thomas enters. He is charming, warm, and immediately at ease.*

Good day, ladies, and may I say how honored I am to be in your fine home. May I present myself to the lady of the house? My name is Thomas O'Brien and I am very lucky to be the friend of Mr. Henry Grey…who is reluctant to enter without an introduction as he is a man of great quality and…almost too great reserve.

LIZZY. Please do come in, Mr. O'Brien. I am Mrs. Darcy and you are very welcome to Pemberley.

> *Georgiana tries to leave, Kitty stops her.*

THOMAS. How lovely it is to meet you Mrs. Darcy, and what a pleasant room. *(Noticing the tree.)* Is that a tree in the corner?

LIZZY. It is a popular German custom!

MARY. Yes, Mr. O'Brien, this Christmas the outside has come *in*.

THOMAS. Well good for it! I have never seen such a thing, but it is beautiful and odd and isn't that a perfect combination.

LIZZY. I'm so glad you appreciate it. Perhaps we may learn the opinion of Mr. Grey, should he be so bold as to…enter the room? Mr.…Grey?

THOMAS. *(To the hiding Henry beyond the doorway.)* Henry the moment has arrived…and so should you.

Henry finally emerges and instantly Georgiana brightens.

LIZZY. Mr. Grey. I am Mrs. Darcy. How do you do? We are so happy to welcome you both.

HENRY. Thank you Mrs. Darcy. The honor is mine.

LIZZY. My husband Mr. Darcy will be along shortly. Of course you know…Miss Georgiana Darcy.

Henry bows low. When he rises, their eyes remain locked together and they are unable to speak. So…Lizzy continues, while Georgiana and Henry just stare, awkwardly but also kind of sweetly.

And…these are my sisters, Mrs. Jane Bingley…

JANE. Lovely to meet you.

LIZZY. Mrs. Lydia… *(Doesn't know what to say for her last name.)* Wickham?

LYDIA. *Enchanté, monsieur.*

LIZZY. Miss Mary Bennet. For now.

MARY. Correct. Engaged. Ha!

LIZZY. And Miss Kitty Bennet, whom I believe you have met already.

KITTY. Hello, again, Mr. Grey.

Henry does not respond.

Mr. O'Brien, very nice to meet you sir.

THOMAS. And you! So many of…you!

KITTY. Yes, like wolves, we come in a pack.

LIZZY. Kitty.

KITTY. A joke, my word!

THOMAS. Ah, but there is always a dose of truth in wit, Miss Bennet, I shall beware.

Kitty laughs—maybe howls a little howl? Lizzy quiets her.

LIZZY. Mr. Grey, please tell us about yourself.

THOMAS. Go on, Henry!

A pause. Thomas hits Henry on the arm, snapping him out of it. He blushes.

HENRY. I am…Mr. Henry Grey, which you already know, of course. And I…I… *(Does not know what to say so goes for politeness.)* I thank you for your kind welcome so near the holiday.

…and that's all Henry has to say. Thomas steps in with…

THOMAS. Yes indeed, thank you kindly ladies. It being Boxing Day perhaps we should have presented ourselves wrapped up with a ribbon!

LYDIA. I do appreciate a well-tied ribbon.

KITTY. And I appreciate a gentleman who does not take himself too seriously.

THOMAS. Life is too serious to be taken seriously.

JANE. Tell us, Mr. Grey, how were your travels this morning?

HENRY. Perfectly fine, thank you.

Silence.

THOMAS. The roads were nearly empty, I assume on account of the holiday, and everyone already having gone where they are meant to be. It is the blessing and the curse of being young, single men *(Pointedly, to Kitty.)* with no family obligations.

MARY. We have somewhat the opposite blessing, with family almost too abundant.

THOMAS. Too much family? I had thought that was an impossible notion, except in the case of debt, inheritance, and dinner.

KITTY. *(Laughing.)* You are amusing, Mr. O'Brien.

THOMAS. That is what my mother told me. You're a delight.

KITTY. That is *not* what my mother told me.

Kitty and Thomas are delighted to have met and everyone can tell.

LIZZY. And where is it that you have traveled from, Mr. O'Brien?

THOMAS. From nearby, the Grey estate is not far. It has been some time since I have visited this part of the countryside, and I must say it is everything I remembered it to be. The scenery *(Looking directly at Kitty.)* is most beautiful.

LYDIA. Oh, I find "the country" rather dull.

LIZZY. Lydia.

MARY. He was not actually speaking of the country.

LYDIA. *I know.*

KITTY. *As do I and StopTalkingAboutIt.*

LIZZY. Girls. I'm sure Georgiana and Mr. Grey would like to get a word in as well!

Georgiana and Henry look at each other, paralyzed. Thomas leans in.

THOMAS. *Music, Henry!*

HENRY. *(Bravely.)* Yes! Miss Darcy, you had mentioned in your last letter about a new piece you were working on and—

GEORGIANA. *(Saved!)* Oh, yes, I have been longing to tell you! It is one of the most complicated pieces I have ever attempted, managing the contrapuntal themes so much like Bach, but reaching for the emotion of Beethoven. I am still not certain I shall ever do it justice.

HENRY. I have no doubt that you will. You so thoroughly understand the principles as well as the passion it requires to convey the depth of the piece. I would be most grateful if you would do us all the honor.

THOMAS. Absolutely, I have heard nothing from Henry except of the wonder of your playing, Miss Darcy.

MARY. Oh, yes please!

JANE. Wonderful!

LYDIA. Lord, must we?

LIZZY. Really, we'd all love to hear Georgiana play.

LYDIA. But could it be at least something we could dance to?

JANE. *Lydia!* Sit.

MARY. You're going to be such a good mother.

LIZZY. Georgiana has filled this home with music her entire life. There is no better way to enjoy this fine morning, I think.

Lydia sulks, and Georgiana sits down to play. It is indeed complicated, and beautiful. She plays. Henry is enraptured. He moves to the piano, to be closer to her.

Just then Darcy enters with a glass of brandy and Georgiana abruptly stops playing.

DARCY. Please don't stop on my account.

LIZZY. How wonderful, Georgiana!

JANE. Oh, it was marvelous. Your playing is extraordinary!

LYDIA. Definitely not for dancing.

THOMAS. I can see, or rather hear, why Henry speaks so highly of you. Henry. A word for Miss Darcy?

Henry approaches her, wanting to say everything but only manages…

HENRY. Resplendent.

The room shifts, and an understanding is shared by Georgiana and Henry, and everyone observing. Darcy interrupts the moment.

DARCY. I heard the music and wondered if our guests had arrived. And so they have. Mrs. Darcy, please do me the honor of informing me who is in our sitting room?

LIZZY. Of course, dear, this is Mr. Henry Grey and Mr. Thomas O'Brien. They are guests of Georgiana's.

DARCY. Welcome, Guests of Georgiana's About Whom I Have Not Heard Nearly Enough.

GEORGIANA. Brother.

DARCY. It is through no fault of your own, sir. My sister has decided to surprise me this holiday.

Lizzy tries to save the moment.

LIZZY. And who doesn't love a Christmas surprise! Kitty, would you be so kind as to show the gentlemen upstairs, I am sure they are weary from travel.

THOMAS. Yes, of course. We can't thank you enough for your gracious welcome, Mrs. Darcy, Mr. Darcy. Henry?

HENRY. Yes. Thank you. So very much.

KITTY. This way.

They bow, and Kitty takes Thomas and Henry upstairs. After they exit Lizzy glares and clears her throat at Darcy.

DARCY. I welcomed them, did I not?

Georgiana flushes and runs out of the room. Lizzy yanks Darcy's brandy from him and storms out and after Georgiana.

Scene 4

Later that day. Mary is reading a book contentedly; Jane is sitting comfortably doing needlework. Lydia is pacing, fiddling with things, picking up books and setting them down, sitting then standing again. Silence.

LYDIA. It is too quiet.

Silence. Mary turns a page.

I SAID IT IS TOO QUIET.

Mary and Jane look up.

JANE. Some of us prefer the quiet.

MARY. I certainly do.

LYDIA. Well, I do not. It's terribly boring. I'm terribly bored.

MARY. Lydia.

LYDIA. What?

JANE. This moment. It is not about you.

MARY. Not even a bit.

Jane and Mary exchange a smile and return to their tasks. Beat. Lydia will not be appeased.

LYDIA. Well, that…is unacceptable. Kitty and Georgiana. The two of them, always giggling together.

JANE. No, Lydia.   **MARY.** Do not get involved.

LYDIA. And what of these gentlemen? Why are they here? AND FOR WHOM?

MARY. Lydia.

LYDIA. I'm only curious!

JANE. Sit down, Lydia.

LYDIA. *Nothing happens while sitting!*

> *Georgiana rushes into the room, followed by Lizzy and Kitty, and begins pacing and fretting.*

GEORGIANA. Now I am quite certain that he will never speak to me again.

> *She continues to pace, perhaps building up energy to where she is practically running from one end of the room to the other.*

LIZZY. Georgiana, please.   **KITTY.** Wait wait wait wait—

GEORGIANA. No, it was a disaster. Though my brother promised to be welcoming he did not greet them upon their arrival, reminded them they were uninvited when he did appear, and made it perfectly clear he was more interested in his brandy than their company.

LIZZY. And I will speak to him, I assure you.

KITTY. It can all be mended this evening!

GEORGIANA. Not if it continues in this manner. My brother is only part of the problem.

MARY. What is the other part?

GEORGIANA. *Myself!* I thought that I would see Mr. Grey and we would burst into conversation. But I was speechless.

JANE. In case you did not notice, it seems Mr. Grey had a similar affliction.

LIZZY. Did you not *feel* what happened between you when he asked you to play?

KITTY. The way he looked at you was operatic.

MARY. It was lovely and I despise the opera.

LIZZY. Tell me: How do his letters make you feel?

GEORGIANA. I feel as though he understands me thoroughly, without explanation or apology or expectation. I feel calmed by his steadiness and thrilled by his ideas. I feel I could learn every single part of him and still want to know more.

JANE. Oh,   **LIZZY.** Yes, that's   **MARY.** That sounds
Georgiana.   it.   right.

KITTY. And how did you feel when you saw him?

GEORGIANA. Ever since he walked in the room I have longed to…

LYDIA. Be near him.

  LIZZY. Take his hand.

    MARY. Feel his arms around you?

      GEORGIANA. *(With certainty.)* Yes.

KITTY. You love him.

GEORGIANA. *If* I do, then *what* do I do?

JANE. When I first felt love I thought it was so plain to see, but *he* did not know how I felt. If Mr. Grey is the person you most long to be with, do not hesitate to make him understand, somehow.

GEORGIANA. Yes, good, how.

MARY. A robust discussion of Lamarckian evolution was quite sufficient for me.

    She realizes how odd that sounds.

But probably just for me.

LIZZY. Do not be afraid of voicing your opinion, even if it means pointing out his irresistible yet irritating flaws.

LYDIA. Ensure his reputation is sound, that he is known to be truthful. And ask about his gambling.

JANE. Be honest, with him and with yourself.

KITTY. And for you, Georgiana…music. Always music. It is what first brought you together, it is the language you share. Trust yourself. You will know what to do.

GEORGIANA. Thank you. Is this what it is to have sisters?

LIZZY. Indeed. Sisters will always be there to hold you up, darling.

JANE. We will.

MARY. Whether you want us to or not.

GEORGIANA. And what of my brother?

LIZZY. I shall manage him. Shall we go?

    The sisters rise to leave and chatter as they go. Lydia stops Georgiana on the way out.

LYDIA. I wish I'd had such wisdom before I married. You do not know how fortunate you are.

They share a look, a moment. Kitty calls from offstage.

KITTY. Georgiana?

GEORGIANA. Yes.

She takes Lydia's hand.

We're coming.

Georgiana brings Lydia along, and Lydia is so grateful.

Scene 5

Later that day. Thomas admires/investigates the strange tree. Henry enters anxiously.

THOMAS. Henry, where have you been hiding all afternoon?

HENRY. I was preparing, practicing, so as to do better.

THOMAS. Better than this morning? Not possible. I have never, in the entirety of my life seen anyone so completely steady and calm as you were, friend.

HENRY. I know it was a miserable display. That is why I was practicing!

THOMAS. I do not understand, the entire journey, you have been unable to cease talking of Miss Darcy and then we arrive and…

HENRY. I proceed to become a very convincing figure of a statue.

THOMAS. More of a rabbit on the lawn I think.

HENRY. A rabbit?

THOMAS. Silent and fidgety.

HENRY. Enough! And this is my first acquaintance with her family. I shall never recover.

THOMAS. The ladies will forgive you. Her brother, it seems, will not be so easily won over.

HENRY. I must find a way!

THOMAS. Tell him you adore her and will stop at nothing to care for her. That is all that older brothers long to hear.

HENRY. And that is all I long to say! I do adore her! The way she contemplates the world, the way she dreams in music, her passion, her talent! My god, when she plays! And when she writes…to me… I hear in her words…peace. Like I've never known. Which is why I must know if she feels the same. To have come all this way and not tell her…

THOMAS. *Then you should tell her.*

HENRY. I want to but…that would also mean telling her…the rest.

THOMAS. The rest of what?

HENRY. I have not been entirely forthcoming.

THOMAS. Then, by all means, come forth.

HENRY. My brother's mismanagement of our family's estate is far worse than I knew of. He has lost everything.

THOMAS. No!

HENRY. Yes, this letter details the extent of it, and all was confirmed when I spoke with my father. The estate will be sold, my family name will be as good as dust. I must leave Oxford.

He hands Thomas the letter.

THOMAS. No! If *you* are unable to complete your studies, I fear what will happen to my own. You're the only reason I understand half of what I'm meant to. It would seem your brother has ensured the failure of us both! But Henry, what will you do?

HENRY. I shall go to London, and I shall work, and begin a life very much unlike the one I had planned.

THOMAS. My friend, I will help you in any way I can, you must know that.

HENRY. I do but I cannot accept your charity. And there is more.

THOMAS. More?

HENRY. In that same letter, detailing my family shame, my father presented me with an alternative solution. In my absence from home, he has made an arrangement between myself and a young lady. Our families have known each other since before we were born, and to many minds there is no question about the match. She is an only child, stands to inherit everything. The bond would secure our family's debts and allow us to rebuild our reputation. She is an agreeable girl, but—

THOMAS. She is not Miss Darcy.

HENRY. No. I would marry Miss Darcy this moment if I knew her heart. But when she learns of my family, what will she feel then? These things cannot be concealed for long and I needed to tell her before she found out from rumors or gossip. And even if she does feel what I hope she does, would her brother allow it? If there is even a chance, then I will tell my father and mother that I cannot marry.

THOMAS. Ask her. Right away. Tell her everything, most importantly tell her what is in your heart, your desire for her hand.

HENRY. Ask for her hand? Now?

THOMAS. My friend, you have been corresponding with Miss Darcy for nearly a year. Why not ask her to marry? You love her. She loves you!

HENRY. Firstly, how do you know that?! Secondly, even if she does, it does not matter if I cannot provide for her.

THOMAS. She is wealthier than anyone you know!

HENRY. That is not why I seek her favor and I do not want either her or Mr. Darcy thinking so. He has obvious expectations of the man his sister will marry. What do I have to offer?

THOMAS. You have your kindness, your brilliance, your potential. That is all any young lady wants.

HENRY. I had hoped to have had more time, to become the man she deserves. But then this letter arrived and I find myself here, unable to determine how to proceed. I fear now I have drawn you into this as well.

THOMAS. You may draw me into anything, friend. I'm having a lovely time.
(Setting the letter down to take Henry by the shoulders.) Be not fearful, Henry. You are remarkable, and if her inability to take her eyes from yours is any indication, she already thinks as much. Simply say what is in your heart.

Henry begins to speak…

To her. Say it *to her*, not to me. To *her.* Besides, what do you have to lose? Your brother has already lost it all.

HENRY. You are not as amusing as you think you are.

THOMAS. Oh, I certainly am.

Kitty enters.

KITTY. Oh, you certainly are. Good evening, gentlemen.

THOMAS. Miss Bennet! How lovely to see you. We were just discussing how amusing I am!

HENRY. Debatable.

KITTY. Do you disagree, Mr. Grey?

HENRY. There are larger issues at hand!!!

Henry panics, and exits leaving the letter from his parents on the table.

KITTY. Oh. I do hope Mr. Grey is all right?

THOMAS. He will be. Surely. Hopefully.

KITTY. And how are you faring at Pemberley, Mr. O'Brien?

THOMAS. Well, I think. I was hoping that you might indulge me in a tour of the grounds before dinner?

KITTY. I'd be delighted. It really is beautiful.

THOMAS. As are you, Miss Bennet. If I may say so.

KITTY. I shall allow it. You charm me, sir. And, if I may say, I like it very much.

THOMAS. Well, that was the intention. Will you permit me to call on you? Often? And write? And dine? And whatever else you will allow me to bore you with?

KITTY. I am amenable to the idea.

THOMAS. You are? Well, isn't that tremendous! I'm delighted.

KITTY. That was the intention. And now that it is settled, should we not set our sights on Georgiana and Henry, as they are certainly in the greatest need.

THOMAS. They have not gotten off to a very strong start. Is it not because of her brother? He seems a rather foreboding presence.

KITTY. Georgiana is guided by Mr. Darcy in all things, but in this moment she is also guided by her own fear.

THOMAS. Fear? Of Henry? He's the most extraordinary gentleman, excellent friend, handsome, intelligent, ambitious.

KITTY. No, no she obviously loves Henry, she's afraid of what that means.

THOMAS. It means that they must unite! Henry can talk of nothing but Miss Darcy…except when he is actually in the company of Miss Darcy.

KITTY. And she is the same! But love…it was not kind to her in the past. And her brother will not let her forget it.

THOMAS. Oh well, yes of course. Love can be brutal.

KITTY. Terrible thing, love.

THOMAS. Just awful.

KITTY. Why does anyone bother?

THOMAS. Haven't a clue. *(Cuteness.)* Miss Bennet, I am resolved to conspire alongside you.

KITTY. Conspire to what end?

THOMAS. You care for her and I care for him and they care for each other and thus we must have them engaged. If you encourage her and I encourage him, I would be willing to wager on it being settled before the new year.

KITTY. And if you can keep pace with me I would wager it shall happen before the end of the day tomorrow.

THOMAS. But what is to be the prize for which one of us is right?

KITTY. When I win, I shall require you to pledge your enduring love to me.

THOMAS. Ah, and when I win I shall insist that you permit me to speak to your father.

They are both enjoying this immensely.

KITTY. Well then, we seem to have an accord.

THOMAS. We do indeed. Shall we walk?

KITTY. Indeed, we shall.

Scene 6

Later, just before dinner.

Georgiana enters, goes to the piano.

She does not press the keys so as not to draw attention to herself, but she practices nonetheless, floating her fingers about the keys and imagining the notes in her head.

Henry enters, sees her—

HENRY. Oh my, Miss Darcy, I do apologize, I did not expect anyone else to be down already.

GEORGIANA. I was practicing. It settles my mind.

HENRY. Were you? I did not hear.

GEORGIANA. Oh, not out loud. I can hear the notes without playing them. My mind so often turns to music, I have learnt to play silently as I fear I am quite the nuisance otherwise.

HENRY. I do not see how you possibly could be.

GEORGIANA. You are too kind, sir. I am so glad for that. And so glad that you are here.

HENRY. *(Trying to be brave.)* Miss Darcy, may I…

He bails.

Ask what you were playing? In your mind?

GEORGIANA. Oh. Yes. Bach's *Goldberg* Variations.

HENRY. Bach! The brilliance of following not only the melody but the harmonic structures.

GEORGIANA. Exactly. The mathematical theory he invokes to explore mood and tone is enchanting.

HENRY. Utterly. Enchanting.

GEORGIANA. It stirs my mind to try to think the way Bach does.

HENRY. And yet *I* long to hear what *you* think, Miss Darcy. *Musically.*

GEORGIANA. I fear there is no place in this world for my musical voice.

HENRY. And what a loss that is. Especially for those of us who cannot bear the thought of a single day without…

> *He means her but says:*

Music.

GEORGIANA. A day without music is one gone too soon. I have played all my life and I never tire of the moment that sound becomes song. It is the same manner as when words become poetry.

HENRY. And when acquaintance becomes affection.

GEORGIANA. Yes. Something extraordinary born from something so simple.

> *She is overcome and moves toward him or reaches for his hand. This is it; this is the moment.*

HENRY. Miss Darcy, I wonder if I might ask you…in fact, there is something I must tell you. But I am afraid I have lost the ability to sensibly express myself.

GEORGIANA. You can tell me anything, Mr. Grey. In our letters, I have shared many confessions of my own.

HENRY. And to repay you with anything less would be unthinkable. I have just learned of…a change to my circumstances. I wonder, Miss Darcy, what you will think of me, though you must know, I would do anything to remain in your favor.

GEORGIANA. You are always in my favor.

HENRY. Which honors me to no end. And compels me to…

GEORGIANA. Compels you to…?

> *Georgiana thinks he's going to propose, she's giddy. He is trying to confess his ruin. Henry suddenly realizes what she thinks, panics, and bails on the conversation altogether, abruptly pulling back. Which makes her pull back.*

HENRY. To…fear that your brother would not approve of our being found like this: alone, together.

GEORGIANA. Can one be alone, together? We are simply two friends discussing…Bach.

> *What does she mean by "friends"? Georgiana is now doubting his affection at the same time that he is doubting hers.*
> *Jane and Mary enter, followed by Kitty and Thomas.*

HENRY. Of course. Friends. Is what we are. There could be no possible objection to that. Excuse me.

> *Henry moves away and goes to Thomas.*

THOMAS. *(Aside to Henry.)* What's the matter, Henry?

HENRY. *(Aside to Thomas.)* Possibly everything. She said we were friends!

THOMAS. Which is good! Friends is good!

HENRY. Not if I wish to ask for her hand! I still have no clarity as to her mind.

THOMAS. Then tell her yours!

> *Lydia enters just in time to hear…*

HENRY. I tried! I failed! And if I cannot tell her the truth of my circumstances, how could I ever tell her I love her?

THOMAS. You came here with a purpose, Henry. Do not waver in your resolve. If you are engaged to marry, let it be to the woman you truly love. Will you defy that letter or will you deny your heart?

> *Thomas and Henry strategize in the corner.*

> *Lydia moves away, finds the letter laying on the table nearby, picks it up, and exits reading.*

> *Mary approaches Georgiana at the piano.*

MARY. Rather a lot isn't it?

GEORGIANA. Oh dear. Do I look overwhelmed?

MARY. You look…like you are clinging to the piano.

GEORGIANA. It is the only thing that never disappoints me.

MARY. You play wonderfully, you know. The piece you played earlier today. That was one of yours, was it not? That you composed.

GEORGIANA. Oh that was just a small piece, for me really, please do not tell anyone. Only Kitty knows that I…compose. And Henry.

MARY. I promise, as long as you promise you will continue to create music. You are too talented. It was truly a breathtaking piece.

GEORGIANA. Did you really like it?

MARY. Unlike many among our company, I do not know how to lie. Promise me.

GEORGIANA. I promise. And thank you, Mary.

> *Darcy and Lizzy enter, Thomas alerts Henry, who stands and tries to engage with him.*

HENRY. Mr. Darcy, sir. I wish to convey my deep honor to be in your fine home.

DARCY. The honor is mine sir, I am grateful you would travel all this way.

HENRY. I would travel any distance for… *(Was going to say Georgiana.)* …the opportunity to make your acquaintance.

DARCY. And yet I am not the one with whom you have been acquainted for the better part of a year.

HENRY. I…yes…well, Miss Darcy had not yet extended the invitation to meet you.

DARCY. A gentleman would know that it is not entirely her responsibility. Now, tell me more of yourself, sir. Where is your family from? And what exactly are your intentions—

> *Lizzy jumps in to help!*

LIZZY. Georgiana, remind us how you and Mr. Grey met. It was at a concert, was it not?

GEORGIANA. A small salon. A recital at most. A few pieces, nothing grand.

THOMAS. And yet it was the grandest night of your life, was it not Henry?

HENRY. Absolutely.

> *Everyone heard that. Georgiana is instantly red-cheeked.*

DARCY. Certainly, you must agree that grandeur is less important than decorum, which might have dictated you contact a young lady's guardian before engaging in correspondence with someone of her standing. Do you regularly defy decorum?

GEORGIANA. *Brother.*

KITTY. Perhaps Georgiana should play the piece from that night. They shall recreate their first meeting for you, and you shall then be perfectly satisfied with the decorum of it. Georgiana, go!

> *Georgiana rushes to the piano and begins to play quickly before he can answer. It's a lovely piece. She plays it expertly. Everyone shuts up and takes it in. It ends with some amount of flourish.*

And then Georgiana stood up, and Mr. Grey walked over. I was standing just here.

> *She pauses, and in a moment Georgiana jumps into place, Thomas shoves Henry up too. Kitty is having the best time. This should all happen very quickly.*

Then Mr. Grey complimented her playing.

> *She looks at him pointedly.*

HENRY. I…enjoyed your playing?

KITTY. And she said thank you.

GEORGIANA. *(Turning to him.)* Thank you.

KITTY. And they had a short conversation about some complicated music interval that no one else in the world would understand or find interesting.

GEORGIANA. It was interesting!

HENRY. The mathematics of contrapuntal musical harmonies are always interesting.

KITTY. Uh-huh. And then Mr. Grey asked if he could write to her about her playing, and she smiled, and he bowed, and they parted ways.

> *Georgiana and Henry smile and bow to each other, finding this all quite silly and feeling ridiculous at being the center of the room.*

And that was the entirety of the exchange and thus concludes this evening's entertainment. Thank you for your kind attention, all.

THOMAS. BRAVA.

> *Kitty nudges Georgiana to bow to the audience, and Henry,*

nudged by Thomas, does the same. The room erupts in laughter and applause. Mr. Darcy is less amused.

LIZZY. Wonderful! My compliments to the performers!

Lydia rushes in and heads for Darcy.

JANE. Oh, Lydia you just missed the most charming little reenactment.

LYDIA. I do not care for amateur theatrics. Mr. Darcy, I wish to speak to you.

Darcy goes to her.

DARCY. What is it?

LYDIA. I believe there may be more to Mr. Grey than he has revealed.

DARCY. What more?

LYDIA. That is for you to decide. I would not feel right keeping the contents of this letter hidden. And neither should Mr. Grey.

Lydia hands Henry's letter to Darcy.

DARCY. There's always a letter.

And he's gone. Georgiana moves to the piano, joined by Kitty.

GEORGIANA. My brother promised to be kind and appears incapable of keeping his word.

KITTY. Mr. Darcy will come around about Mr. O'Brien. I mean Mr. Grey. I mean—

GEORGIANA. What *do* you mean? And where did you disappear to? When you came in your cheeks were pink!

KITTY. A stroll around the grounds with Mr. O'Brien, that is all.

Pause.

GEORGIANA. Kitty? Kitty! What is that smile? Do you care for him?!

KITTY. I care for nothing more than a walk in the winter air! It is lovely and exhilarating and tall and handsome and makes me laugh.

GEORGIANA. The winter air sounds like it would make a fine husband.

KITTY. We have all the time in the world to discuss the weather;

in this moment, let us direct our attention to Mr. Grey and determine what the future holds for the both of you.

Across the room…

THOMAS. We have come all this way, Henry. You must take advantage and speak your truth, now or not at all. You love her, come out and say it!

HENRY. I cannot! Not in front of her family! Not when I have only ever written to her of music!

THOMAS. Ah, but for the two of you, writing of music is writing of love. You must tell her right now.

HENRY. I cannot. Just give her this poem I have written.

THOMAS. You wrote a poem! I didn't think of a poem! Good man, that'll do it.

HENRY. Then please give it to her and implore her to read it.

THOMAS. With you just across the room?

HENRY. Yes.

THOMAS. No! I am not the Royal Mail! Go over there and read it to her yourself.

HENRY. I cannot! My heart will not let me.

THOMAS. Well, mine will.

He reads Henry's letter aloud.

"For Miss Darcy, from the desk of Mr. Henry Grey."

HENRY. What are you doing? Thomas. Stop it.

THOMAS. "You alone are the source of the music that fills my heart."

HENRY. Lower your voice!

KITTY. What's this?

Georgiana has heard them and rises from her piano.

THOMAS. "Your voice is the melody that draws me in.
Your heart is the rhythm of the song we share."

HENRY. Thomas, please stop.

GEORGIANA. Please don't.

Henry sees his chance and takes the poem back from Thomas and reads his own words aloud.

HENRY. "Like notes become music,
Alone then together.
Silent, then sung.
To begin the refrain.
Is to carry anew.
My wish, my hope,
For a song that will never end."

Georgiana starts playing her piano, accompanying the letter, adding music to it until it is almost a song.

"We are met in harmony.
I need nothing in this life
So much as I need you
By my side,
Happily by yours
Together
Forever."

Georgiana resolves her piano accompaniment.
Henry cannot believe he said that all aloud.

GEORGIANA. Henry.

HENRY. Georgiana, I—I—

GEORGIANA. I know. Now I know.

Before they can even touch hands, Darcy enters explosively.

DARCY. You will not.

GEORGIANA. Brother.

LIZZY. Darling?

DARCY. My suspicions have been confirmed, move away from my sister.

KITTY. Mr. Darcy.

DARCY. The extravagance of his false poetry, his brazen visit to our home, it confirms everything. You, sir, are a scoundrel.

GEORGIANA. *Fitzwilliam.*

THOMAS. Mr. Darcy, no.

LIZZY. Darling, stop this.

MARY. What on earth does he mean?

DARCY. His family is in ruin, he is after her fortune and is determined to steal her away.

GEORGIANA. Brother, no, please.

THOMAS. With all respect, Mr. Darcy, you do not know this man.

DARCY. That is precisely the point. None of us do. This man has deceived you, Georgiana! Has he told you he must leave Oxford for London in the new year, forced to work?

MARY. Is having to work really so offensive?

DARCY. It is if you lie about it! *(To Georgiana.)* Unless he has told you that his once reputable family has lost their estate, that it was lost through reckless mismanagement, that he has nothing to offer you—unless he has told you all this, he has not been honest.

HENRY. Sir, I will admit to your charges but that is not the full story. I came straight away, as soon as I learned of it.

DARCY. Gentlemen, I hope you will understand when I implore you to depart this instant.

LIZZY. Mr. Darcy, I urge you to calm yourself.

GEORGIANA. Please do not do this!

HENRY. Sir, you must first allow me to explain.

DARCY. Then please start by explaining your *fiancée.*

    GASP.

MARY. What?

  KITTY. Fiancée.

    GEORGIANA. Henry?

      JANE. Oh, my word.

THOMAS. No, that's not the truth of it at all.

DARCY. You speak of the truth, when we have been lied to from the very first.

GEORGIANA. Henry, what is all this?

HENRY. Georgiana, this is not how I would have had you learn of it.

THOMAS. It is not his choice.

DARCY. Then you admit to the arrangement and to withholding the truth from my sister! Perhaps the reason you chose to write to her only of music was because to speak honestly would have meant revealing your engagement to another woman.

HENRY. It is true that an arrangement was made—

> **GEORGIANA.** But the arrangement has ended. You ended it, did you not?

> > **HENRY.** I…am going to—

> > > **DARCY.** Do you see? The duplicity!

GEORGIANA. You are engaged? Henry, I do not understand.

HENRY. I came here to confirm your feelings.

DARCY. You came here, wagering you could lure my sister in so as to steal her fortune, all while keeping another woman waiting in case your schemes were not successful.

KITTY. No.

THOMAS. That is not his motive!

HENRY. No—that is not at all—no—

LIZZY. Mr. Darcy, stop.

DARCY. I will not stop when my sister's future is at stake. How do you hope to earn her love if you lie to her?

GEORGIANA. Brother, let him speak!

HENRY. I did not lie.

DARCY. Omission is the worst kind of lie. *(To Georgiana.)* You will have no more contact with this man who has proven himself unworthy. I forbid it.

> *Lizzy gasps. It is over. Georgiana is heartbroken.*

GEORGIANA. Henry, you could have told me.

HENRY. I am
heartsick
to have
failed you.
(To Darcy.) And you sir. I never meant to—

DARCY. Leave. Sir.

Henry and Thomas look at each other. Henry is devastated,
addresses Lizzy.

HENRY. Yes. Of course. My apologies, Mrs. Darcy, Mr. Darcy, and…Miss Darcy.

Henry leaves, heartbroken, barely able to look at Georgiana
one last time.

GEORGIANA. HENRY.

Georgiana runs to Henry, still not sure what to say to him.

DARCY. *(A warning.)* Georgiana.

HENRY. I fear that too much has been broken. I am…so terribly sorry.

Henry loves her so much but tears himself away and exits.

Kitty runs to Georgiana to comfort her.

Thomas follows Henry, turning at the door.

THOMAS. Deepest apologies, Mrs. Darcy.

He turns to leave, but pauses.

And Miss Bennet, I—

Kitty looks at him, wants to go to him, but stays with Geor-
giana, who needs her more.

KITTY. Goodbye Mr. O'Brien.

THOMAS. Goodbye.

And the guests are gone. Shock.
Georgiana is unsure whether to weep or rage.

DARCY. I am sorry for this outcome, sister, but I know you will come to see it rightly. He was dishonest. He has nothing. I have saved you from ruin. Again.

GEORGIANA. Enough! Enough, brother. I am more ruined now than I ever could have been. You have assured with your severity, that neither my love nor his matters.

DARCY. He was engaged!

GEORGIANA. As were you, before Lizzy! You did not let him explain!

DARCY. If he could have proven himself he would have.

GEORGIANA. You. Do not. Know him. You never gave him a chance; you distrusted him before he even arrived.

How could anyone ever consider me, when with me comes a lifetime of inquiry and scrutiny and examination from you? How could anyone survive *you*?

Georgiana collapses into Kitty, who holds her. Lizzy goes to them too, shooting daggers at Darcy, who looks as though he has suddenly realized that he has gone too far.

KITTY. Darling.

DARCY. Georgiana, you must know—

GEORGIANA. *Leave me, brother. Please go.*

LIZZY. Leave us, dear. Please.

Darcy leaves.

Darling, do not despair.

GEORGIANA. But I do. I do.

Suddenly Thomas is back, he runs to Kitty.

THOMAS. Miss Bennet…

For once she doesn't know what to say.

Will she be all right?

KITTY. I do not know. Will he?

THOMAS. I do not know. *(Wants to say more, adores her so, and thus is suddenly open and earnest.)* Miss Bennet, I could not depart without confirming my most ardent wish to call on you in the new year. If that might yet be agreeable?

It is agreeable to her, but she must tend to her friend.

KITTY. Mr. O'Brien… I…

you must go now, please.

THOMAS. Yes, of course. Until we meet again, Miss Bennet.

KITTY. Until then.

He holds her hand—which is just simple magic. He exits.

Georgiana is surrounded by the Bennet sisters, and is one of them.

LYDIA. It was very much not my intention but…did I ruin every-thing? I found the letter, I gave it to Mr. Darcy.

KITTY. YOU WHAT.

    MARY. Lydia, you didn't.

        JANE. We told you not to intervene!

            LIZZY. You know how Mr. Darcy is.

                LYDIA. I thought I was helping. I meant to help!

                    KITTY. *You meant to find a way to leap into the middle of everyone else's lives, as you always do!*

GEORGIANA. No. Kitty, no, this is not her fault.

    She takes Lydia's hand.

It is my brother's. He will always make happen only and exactly what is best for *him.*

LIZZY. Perhaps if Mr. Darcy were to write to Mr. Grey and—

GEORGIANA. His prejudice will never let him. His pride would dry the ink before it left his pen.

    Georgiana rises and goes to the piano. She lays Henry's poem atop the blank music pages resting there.

But that is not true for the ink drawn from mine. From this moment on.

I. Will not. Be quiet.

    She holds fast to her sisters.

    Blackout.

End of Act One

ACT TWO

Prologue

Letters, of course.

But we are now…six years later, 1821.

Georgiana, now in her early twenties, is confident, winsome and wise.

Kitty, also in her early twenties, is the happiest, energetic and proud.

GEORGIANA. Dearest Kitty,
You must find the time to call; there is much to do. We are entering a new era in which women must perform, conduct, and even compose without compromise. If the Royal Society won't admit women musicians, then we shall create a society of our own to show the world exactly what we are capable of, and we will do it together! We shall announce The Society for Women Musicians with a concert at my home in London this Christmas Eve!

KITTY. At last the vision you have for women and music is born! And on Christmas Eve! There will be much to do but what a joy to do it. We shall announce the Society, you will play the latest George Williams. The invitations have been sent.

> *Letters fade into a scene.*

GEORGIANA. Excellent! And you must share remarks that will inspire benefactors to fund the group.

KITTY. The patrons do not want to hear from me, they want to hear from you!

GEORGIANA. On the contrary, you are so much better with people. I may be able to play, but you, my friend, are persuasive!

KITTY. Together, there is nothing we cannot do.

GEORGIANA. It is exhilarating! We shall— *(Switching tone.)* Sorry, invitations are sent? To whom?

KITTY. Oh! Friends, family, everyone. *(Realizing.)* Which means my sister.

GEORGIANA. Which means my brother.

Smash to Lizzy reading the invitation, Darcy fuming, sputtering with outrage.

LIZZY. "Georgiana Darcy requests the pleasure of your company at eight o'clock on Christmas Eve for a concert of new piano compositions by George Williams at her home in London, to honor the debut of The Society for Women Musicians. A reply is requested."

DARCY. What on earth is she doing? A musical society? Of women? It's barely appropriate for them to perform publicly, much less organize en masse. And at Christmas no less! Georgiana has no husband, lives alone, stays out every evening playing concerts for god knows who, and now this!

LIZZY. We're going.

DARCY. We most certainly are not. That is the Darcy name and our family fortune she is using to sow disorder!

LIZZY. Which means it is her name and fortune to do with as she likes. She's your sister. I'm your wife.
We are going.

Blackout.

<h1 style="text-align:center">Scene 1</h1>

London, December 24th, late morning, in Georgiana's handsomely appointed home. Georgiana enters in something comfortable and goes to her piano. We are no longer at Pemberley, and she is no longer living with her brother.

She goes through letters, calling cards, and notes. It's a lot of mail. Fan mail. It makes her smile.

Kitty enters talking a mile a minute. Kitty is now Georgiana's manager.

KITTY. Look at the attendees for the concert tonight! I've simply never seen a more popular event and I can barely contain my glee at being the person holding the guest list. Anyone who has ever thrown a sideways glance my way shall be stricken from this paper and I shall feel no regret whatsoever.

Kitty suddenly sees a name, strikes it with satisfaction. Georgiana is not listening, but looking through letters, papers.

Oh, Georgie, please do not shuffle those papers around. One lot I meant to reply to and the other I was fully planning to ignore and now I do not recall which was which!

GEORGIANA. *(Referring to one paper in particular.)* It would seem some people do not agree with our cause.

KITTY. They may disagree all they like, but it shall not stop our efforts. The concert will go seamlessly this evening, and so will the debut of the Society.

GEORGIANA. Yes. I hope so.

KITTY. Do you doubt it?

GEORGIANA. I do not doubt us, but I do doubt…most everyone else. We are starting something that necessitates defiance against a world that prefers women remain powerless.

KITTY. And when they hear you play they shall know precisely how wrong they are. It may not be comfortable to change the world, but the world will be better for it. So. Would you like your Christmas present now or later or now?

> *Kitty reveals a small box wrapped in a ribbon and puts it on the piano.*

GEORGIANA. Kitty, no. You shouldn't have.

KITTY. What is a friend for if not to shower you with holiday trinkets.

GEORGIANA. It's not fair to give me a gift when I haven't wrapped your…oh look, yes I have.

> *Georgiana takes out a small gift as well. The friends laugh and open their presents. Kitty opens the box to reveal a lovely little necklace.*

Do you like it?

KITTY. I love it! I love it so much…that I got the exact same necklace for you.

GEORGIANA. What! You did not!

> *Georgiana reveals the same necklace.*

KITTY. From the shop on Regent Street. The shopkeeper told me it was one of a kind!

GEORGIANA. He told me the same! I shall wear it at tonight's concert and think of you.

KITTY. It is difficult to avoid thinking of me as I always sit in front.

GEORGIANA. Kitty. Tonight will be the start of something so very important. Something I could not have dreamt of without you by my side. And with everything else you manage: with your children, your home—

KITTY. My husband, the dog, my husband's family, their dogs— yes it is a lot.

GEORGIANA. And you do it all so well. I am aware of how much is asked of you and how much you devote to me. And…I am so grateful for you.

KITTY. As am I for you. And proud! Look at what we've done! A society of our own! Well more for you really, I can't play a note but

I do so love that you can, and now more women will and soon we shall fill the city with music and women making it!

GEORGIANA. I know we are in the right, but I confess to feeling a bit uneasy.

KITTY. Oh, I'm terrified. But all will be well if we simply keep doing unexpected things with confidence.

> *Thomas enters.*

How do you think I married Thomas?

THOMAS. Kitty, my dear, there you are! Georgiana, Happy Christmas!

GEORGIANA. Happy Christmas, Thomas! We were just talking about you.

THOMAS. Good things I hope.

KITTY. How outlandish it was to marry you.

THOMAS. Ah yes, still can't believe I got away with that. *(To Kitty.)* My darling, you had a task set out for me this morning, did you not?

KITTY. Not one, but several. You were to deliver the gifts to my Aunt and Uncle Gardiner, retrieve the pamphlets for tonight from the printers, and pay a call on the Darcys to tell them and my sisters that we would welcome them for a light supper before the concert. Did you fail, my love?

THOMAS. Spectacularly! I only just left the house to come here. But the boys and I did play a very invigorating game of hide-and-seek.

KITTY. The nanny was to mind the boys while you ran the errands! Honestly, it is as though I have three sons and not two. *(To Georgiana.)* Georgiana, the family *are* welcome for an early dinner, are they not? My sisters? Which includes Lizzy?

GEORGIANA. Of course they are and I suppose Lizzy must be accompanied by her husband.

KITTY. You know I love you, my dear, but you are suffering the same condition as afflicts your brother.

GEORGIANA. And what condition is that?

KITTY. The impressive talent for cultivating a grievance until it borders on spite.

GEORGIANA. Any spite started with his stubborn insistence that he is entitled to an opinion on my life!

KITTY. And your equally stubborn insistence that he is wrong before hearing his opinion!

GEORGIANA. *(Getting angry.)* He denies responsibility for the severity of his actions, believes "love" to mean control and "sister" to mean property, and does not consider anyone's judgment valid but his own. I am happy to forgive him should he become forgivable.

> *Pause.*

THOMAS. What an easy and carefree Christmas this shall be.

KITTY. Thomas, would it be helpful if I wrote these tasks down for you?

THOMAS. *(Looking out the window.)* No need as there is one less task to remember.

KITTY. How do you mean?

THOMAS. The Darcys and your sisters seem to be arriving at this very moment.

KITTY. Thomas, you were meant to tell them to come later!

GEORGIANA. I'll go.

KITTY. No no no, this is your house. I shall find a way to occupy the ladies. Thomas will distract Mr. Darcy for the better part of the morning. Georgiana, you may relax and prepare in your own home.

THOMAS. The only thing I can think to do with Darcy is drink.

KITTY. Godspeed then. Georgiana, ready?

GEORGIANA. As I shall ever be.

> *A bustle at the door as Darcy and Lizzy enter, followed quickly by Jane, Mary, and Lydia. Greetings all around.*

LIZZY. Oh Georgiana! How I have missed you! It feels as though we never see you anymore.

GEORGIANA. I have missed you too, dear sister. Hello!

JANE. Darling Georgiana, thank you for welcoming us to your home.

MARY. Wonderful to see you!

LYDIA. Oh, it is so good to be here.

GEORGIANA. And to have you!

KITTY. Welcome everyone!

DARCY. Happy Christmas, Georgiana.

GEORGIANA. Brother.

LIZZY. Apologies for the early call, but we simply could not wait to see you and the boys!

KITTY. The boys are with the nanny at our home, you and your girls shall see them in the morning. I'm so thrilled that you can all join us in London this Christmas.

LIZZY. I am pleased to be together no matter where we are.

THOMAS. Likewise! Hello, Darcy.

DARCY. O'Brien, Happy Christmas.

THOMAS. Happy Christmas, sir. Your arrival has allowed me to complete one of my errands early so I thought we might visit the club for a drink?

DARCY. A fine plan. After I just walked in the door, no less. You would not be trying to hastily evict me from the premises, would you?

THOMAS. *(Lying terribly.)* Nooooooooo.

GEORGIANA. Hello brother.

DARCY. Sister, how are you?

GEORGIANA. I remain well. And busy. With the new Society.

DARCY. Yes, I have heard. I admit I am quite curious about your new…group.

GEORGIANA. Curious about what?

DARCY. The point.

    JANE. Oh dear.

        MARY. So soon?

            LYDIA. This should be fun!

                LIZZY. We've only just arrived.

GEORGIANA. *(Taking the bait but knowing she will win.)* Music is a universal language. And women should have a voice in all things universal as they are not only participants but creators in this world. Women deserve meaning, and for the women in this Society, music is meaning. If a world ruled by men does not include us, we must create a space for ourselves or else forgo what is universally ours, and that I refuse to do. Music belongs to me just as much as it does to any man. That…is the point.

> *Darcy hears that loud and clear.*

MARY. Well said, Georgiana.

KITTY. That will make an excellent fundraising pamphlet.

DARCY. No one wants to limit your life, but there is a reason things are done the way they are done. I fear what society will say about you.

GEORGIANA. I think you fear *me*.

KITTY. SHALL WE HAVE SOME TEA?

LYDIA. Brilliant idea.

THOMAS. Suddenly very thirsty. Mr. Darcy, shall we enjoy a brandy at the club?

DARCY. It is ten o'clock in the morning!

THOMAS. And a Happy Christmas to us. Ladies.

DARCY. *(Kissing Lizzy.)* Darling. *(Bowing.)* Ladies. *(A loaded glance at Georgiana.)* Sister.

> *Thomas and Darcy exit. The six women settle into comfortable conversation, though Georgiana is still fuming.*

GEORGIANA. Apologies to all. I am sure you are used to the endless bickering between my brother and me, though I fear it becomes tiresome. It certainly is to me.

LIZZY. Oh, darling. Never apologize for speaking your mind. You and your brother are simply very much alike which means neither one will ever sacrifice your belief that you are in the right. And as I love you both dearly, I resign myself to Not. Get. Involved.

GEORGIANA. I am sorry to put you in this position sister.

LIZZY. I would not have it any other way. You once were so silent with your brother, deferring to him in all things. I much prefer you now. It is good for my husband to be challenged, and not just by me.

LYDIA. I do remember how quiet you used to be! Lord, how did we not know this spirited young woman was inside you that whole time!

KITTY. I knew, thank you very much!

LIZZY. Oh, Georgiana, we miss you. You have not been back to Pemberley for the holiday in, what can it be, five years!

GEORGIANA. Six.

MARY. Well, I am perfectly happy to be in London for Christmas. Just having come from South America—by train, on horseback, by boat, and carriage—I will happily stay anywhere so long as I am able to be still at least through the spring.

KITTY. Oh, Mary, your life with Arthur sounds wildly exciting. Do you miss your husband terribly?

MARY. I do. But he will return soon enough to bore you all with tales of flora, fauna, and fungi.

LIZZY. And what will you do in the meantime?

MARY. Read alone and peacefully. Or perhaps write a book on the diversity of gastropods of greater Brazil? I am compiling our research on the subject and find it most invigorating.

LYDIA. Uh-huh. I do hope you will at least have some time for parties?

JANE. As much as she ever had!

MARY. Which is not at all. But I take it your social life is still as lively as always, Lydia?

LYDIA. I simply go where I am invited, which these days is everywhere! I have just returned from the country where I have been staying at the estate of the earl. He relies on me to organize his social calendar which, thanks to me, is quite full.

LIZZY. So you and the earl are still…courting?

LYDIA. We are very very *very* good friends. When his wife died years ago he swore he'd never marry again, but lately he has been hinting he may yet change his mind.

JANE. But are you happy?

LYDIA. Truly!

JANE. That is all that matters to me. Though spare a week from your many parties and come visit your nieces, won't you? They miss their Aunt Lydia.

KITTY. And how are the girls, Jane?

JANE. They confirm that having five daughters is just as tiring and lovely as mother said *we* were. They will join us tomorrow after spending time with the elder Mr. and Mrs. Bingley while my husband returns to the bedside of his dying sister.

LIZZY. She's dying? Again?

JANE. Again. This is the third holiday—two Christmases and my birthday—where illness has suddenly befallen her.

MARY. What a coincidence.

LYDIA. She's not sick.

JANE. Lydia!

LYDIA. Literally everyone is think-ing it!	**MARY.** She's not wrong.	**KITTY.** I mean…	**LIZZY.** Oh Caroline.

JANE. I am learning that being a part of the Bingley family is knowing certain facts without ever uttering them.

> *The women laugh.*

GEORGIANA. Oh, how I love it when we are all together.

JANE. It does not happen nearly enough.

LIZZY. Well, we are here now. And all so proud of you, Georgie.

MARY. So proud! Kitty said the queen herself has heard you play!

LYDIA. She has! And I mention it with such frequency I am now, "Georgiana Darcy's sister" and let me tell you, it serves me very well at parties.

GEORGIANA. I have so much to be thankful for. All of you, all that Kitty and I have built, my music, the new Society.

KITTY. Speaking of which, it is time for you to prepare for the evening, and there is much to do. Lydia, would you be able to entertain everyone for a bit? I'm sure there is some last-minute holiday shopping to be done.

LYDIA. Of course! There is a lovely new dress shop.

MARY. Is it near a bookstore?

LIZZY. We will see you this evening. You'll be wonderful, Georgiana.

> *The sisters all exit, Georgiana and Kitty regroup.*

KITTY. Is there anything else you need before tonight?

GEORGIANA. No, though… I do wonder…if perhaps tonight I should…reveal everything.

KITTY. Tonight?

GEORGIANA. Perhaps.

KITTY. Everything?

GEORGIANA. What do you think?

KITTY. I think…that the Women's Society alone will cause such a stir. Is it prudent to expose yourself so completely?

GEORGIANA. It may not be prudent but it would be proof. Proof that we belong in all places music is played.

KITTY. Of course I agree. But you cannot. I'm sorry. I'm only trying to safeguard what we've built and what it could become.

GEORGIANA. Of course you are.

> *Georgiana exits, leaving Kitty to fret for a moment before kicking into high gear once more.*

Scene 2

> *Early afternoon. Kitty is bustling around the room when Thomas enters, carrying the printed pamphlets for the evening.*

KITTY. There you are! I was worried you became lost! On your way through our neighborhood! Which you live in and are most familiar with!

THOMAS. I was keeping Mr. Darcy occupied with a drink, as you had suggested would be helpful. Not that I minded, as it was a lovely and relaxing way to spend the morning.

KITTY. Oh, I'm so pleased your morning was spent relaxing at the club. Meanwhile, I have been feverishly occupied with all the preparations for the evening. Did you remember to pick up the pamphlets?

THOMAS. I did. And I have them just here.

KITTY. Let me see them. I do like this new printer we are using; the work is so fine.

THOMAS. In fact, the printer has accompanied me and is outside in the hall. He wanted to be entirely sure you were satisfied, and to thank you.

KITTY. On Christmas Eve? Well, he certainly is dedicated to his work. I would love to meet him finally.
Please, show him in.

THOMAS. *(Going to the door, grinning.)* Sir, the moment has arrived, and so should you.

> *In walks Henry Grey, more confident and at ease than before. He is carrying a folio.*

HENRY. Mrs. O'Brien, how lovely to see you again.

> *Kitty is speechless. Thomas is practically bouncing with delight.*

THOMAS. Darling, you remember—

KITTY. *(Shooting him a look.)* Of course I do, Thomas. Mr. Grey, hello! What a surprise to see you.

HENRY. I apologize for the interruption to your day.

KITTY. No, no. You are…very welcome. I'm sorry, I must say I am somewhat shocked to learn that you are in fact our printer.

HENRY. I certainly did not intend to deceive. I have worked at Hartford Printing for nearly five years, until I recently took over as one of the owners—we are soon to become Hartford and Grey Printing and Publishing.

THOMAS. Isn't that wonderful!

KITTY. Mr. Grey, let me congratulate you on all your success.

HENRY. We are doing fairly well.

THOMAS. Hartford and Grey is earning its reputation as one of the most innovative and influential publishing houses in London, all due to Henry's ambition and vision of course.

HENRY. I saw an opportunity, and am fortunate there is an appetite.

You see, I have longed to expand our business to include publishing novels, plays, and music scores—music being my personal priority. Through Thomas I learned of all you and Miss Darcy were doing.

THOMAS. I did you both a favor by bringing your interests together! Kitty's Society will introduce a new era in music. You need each other and you're welcome!

KITTY. Thank you, but it is not my Society alone, of course.

HENRY. Of course, I have had the pleasure of hearing Miss Darcy's interpretations of George Williams several times over the past few years. I have always been awestruck at the intricacy of the composition and the genius of her playing.

KITTY. You have seen her play?

HENRY. As often as I was able.

KITTY. And were you accompanied? By your wife?

HENRY. Ah. No. When I decided to move to London, my brother married the young lady who was my intended, and they are now the parents of four beautiful children and shockingly quite happy.

KITTY. I see.

THOMAS. And good for them!

HENRY. When Thomas told me of your Society, I thought I could finally do more than applaud in the dark. To that end, Mrs. O'Brien, Hartford and Grey would like to offer our patronage and support the Society with the printing of anything you need, at no cost.

KITTY. Mr. Grey, that is very generous of you!

THOMAS. Truly! *(To Kitty.)* I did not know he was going to do that. *(To Henry.)* Henry, that is too kind! You must join us tonight! Your presence would go a long way to establish the Society's legitimacy! Don't you agree, Kitty?

HENRY. I was also hoping to show appreciation to Miss Darcy directly—I have a gift.

KITTY. Unfortunately, the concert is completely full. I'm so sorry to disappoint you.

HENRY. *(Terribly disappointed.)* Yes. And of course I did not come here today expecting an invitation.

KITTY. Perhaps another time, Mr. Grey.

HENRY. Of course.

> *Pause.*

Then I'll wish you all the very best success tonight. Thomas.

THOMAS. Henry.

> *Henry bows and exits. Kitty whirls on Thomas.*

KITTY. You will explain.

THOMAS. After you! You turn him away?!

KITTY. Yes I did, it's too much. This is a critical evening and Georgiana needs her entire mind focused. What would happen if she looks up and sees Mr. Grey in the fifth row?

THOMAS. He's an old friend, not a surprise attack.

KITTY. He is more than a friend to her and you know it. I cannot allow it.

THOMAS. Could you not ask her instead of presuming she would be so unsteadied by his presence?

KITTY. Not when even asking could upset her!

THOMAS. You make her sound like some helpless, delicate rose!

KITTY. Roses are surprisingly hardy flowers!

THOMAS. Then whose point are you proving?! He wants to help! Free printing! A patron of the Society!

KITTY. I do not care what he wants! You brought Mr. Grey to Georgiana's home on the day of the most important concert of her life. And what is more, you have been his regular companion, all these years?

THOMAS. Henry was my friend before he ever met Georgiana. Am I not allowed to maintain our friendship because of what happened at Pemberley?

KITTY. Do not claim to believe your continued friendship with Henry Grey had no consequence on anyone else in this family.

THOMAS. I know him. He has followed her music, attended her concerts, and has offered his support. He belongs here tonight.

KITTY. *This was to be the debut of the Society not the debut of*

Mr. and Mrs. Grey. We have one chance; London will not give us another. You might think that's less interesting than a courtship but I do not.

THOMAS. Does it have to be only one or the other? Could it not be both?

KITTY. Could it not have waited until tomorrow?!

THOMAS. He wants to see her. How do you know she does not want to see him?

KITTY. *I know what she wants better than she does!*

THOMAS. I love you but having a hand in every part of someone else's life does remind me somewhat of *your sister.*

> *Knowing he means Lydia, which infuriates Kitty of course:*

KITTY. Which. One.

THOMAS. Which one indeed.

> *They both exit in different directions, so angry.*

Scene 3

> *Early afternoon. Georgiana is practicing when Mr. Darcy enters. He is surprised to find her alone. He listens to her play for a moment, thinking she does not know he is there, when, while continuing to play...*
>
> *During the scene Georgiana may use the piano to articulate her frustration—note, chords, or percussive taps like punctuation for her feelings.*

GEORGIANA. Do you need something, brother?

DARCY. I did not mean to interrupt you.

GEORGIANA. You did not. I can play while you are here.

DARCY. Yes, well. We so rarely get to speak anymore.

GEORGIANA. Because every time we speak we argue, as you willfully choose to misunderstand me.

DARCY. I'd like to understand.

GEORGIANA. Would you? As you have made abundantly clear, the life I have made for myself, you do not approve. And never will, it would seem.

DARCY. I only wished for a life for you filled with marriage, comfort, children, happiness.

GEORGIANA. The life you have, you mean.

DARCY. Is my life not to your liking?

GEORGIANA. It is your life, brother. I do not have to like it. Just as my life pleases me and no longer requires approval from you.

DARCY. I was protecting you. I am protecting you.

GEORGIANA. And in so doing you prevent me from having that perfect life you expected of me.

DARCY. I have apologized!

GEORGIANA. *(As if that could ever be enough.)* You may apologize to me every day, dear brother, but you will never change. You continue to assume you know what is best for me.

DARCY. How are you so certain I am wrong, sister? I do not think you appreciate all I have done to secure your future, your fortune.

GEORGIANA. My fortune is my right by law, my future is one I have made for myself, what part have you played in either?

DARCY. You resist convention and I believe it is to spite me. Or perhaps to punish me.

GEORGIANA. I do not resent you. But I will not allow you to judge the life I built from the ruins you created.

> *They square off, neither willing to give an inch.*
> *Lizzy enters, bustling with last-minute Christmas shopping energy.*

LIZZY. Oh, good, you are both here. I have chosen a few small trinkets for… *(Takes the temperature of the room.)* Oh, did I interrupt the end or the beginning of the fight?

DARCY. Hello darling. Would you be so kind as to remind my sister that I have her best interests at heart?

GEORGIANA. Sister, would you please suggest to my brother that he keep his heart, questionable that it even exists, away from the affairs of my own?

LIZZY. Georgiana, I know Christmas is a particularly hard time for you—

GEORGIANA. Oh no, I love Christmas! At least I did until my brother decided to ruin it for me.

DARCY. I did no such thing!

LIZZY. Mr. Darcy, denying the events of the past does not make them go away.

DARCY. At some point, I must be forgiven!

GEORGIANA. One cannot demand to be forgiven. That is not how forgiveness works.

LIZZY. If you both would please lower your voices—

DARCY. *(Shouting.)* My voice is the perfect volume!

GEORGIANA. *(Also shouting.)* And I will be as loud as I like in my own home!

LIZZY. *(Roaring.)* I only meant that everyone else was just behind me!

> *All three are out of breath and glaring at one another when the door opens and Kitty ushers in Jane, Mary, and Lydia.*

GEORGIANA. *Good day, brother.*

DARCY. *And good day to you.*

> *Georgiana storms off one way and Darcy bows hastily and exits out the front door.*

MARY. And yet it does not sound altogether good at all.

JANE. Oh, Lizzy.

LIZZY. Honestly, those two. We will never have a happy Christmas again. Next year I will cancel it altogether and join Mr. de Bourgh wherever he is on his travels, the farther away the better.

MARY. I honestly love that idea.

LYDIA. Or we could visit Anne de Bourgh—she and her good friend Cecily have all that room, just the two of them in that great house and all their unusual friends!

LIZZY. Do not tempt me.

KITTY. Georgiana is simply on edge because of the concert tonight.

MARY. It truly is wonderful what you are doing Kitty. I, for one, look forward to hearing more from women musicians and composers. I love Beethoven but it is a mood, is it not?

LYDIA. I do not mean to interrupt, but, well, I am going to. I was out with the earl, and he wanted to stop to look in on the invitations for the ball we're hosting for Twelfth Night and we walked into the printers and who do you imagine was right there, plain as day, behind the counter. Mr. Henry Grey! Can you imagine?!?!

LIZZY. No! Mr. Grey is in London?

JANE. I had always wondered what happened to him.

LYDIA. What happened is that he owns the whole publishing house! He is terribly successful and exceedingly handsome and, upon subtle inquiry, found to be unmarried! Had I not been with my dear earl I just might have—

KITTY. *Do not finish that.*

LIZZY. Kitty, did you know?

KITTY. Not until earlier this very day. Not only has Thomas remained friends with Mr. Grey these six years without my knowledge but he had Georgiana and I recently engage him as our printer! Again, without my knowledge! My dear husband did not see fit to tell me until this morning, when he decided to bring Mr. Grey by the house for a visit! Surprise!

LIZZY. No! Did Georgiana see him?

KITTY. Thankfully no, but Thomas then invited Mr. Grey to the concert this evening putting all that we've worked for at risk. And I…I told him not to come.

LYDIA. You what?!

MARY. Why?!

LIZZY. Was that fair, Kitty?

KITTY. Georgiana must think only of the Williams tonight, only of the Society, she cannot do that if she sees Mr. Grey.

MARY. Georgiana is one of the foremost pianists in London; she could be playing within a hailstorm and would scarcely notice the rain. Seeing a man would never unmoor her that far, would it?

JANE. But Mr. Grey is not just any man.

KITTY. Thank you! We do not have time for love.

LYDIA. Um…Georgiana might!

KITTY. Well, it's too late now! He's not coming!

> *The sisters all share a glance.*

LIZZY. Kitty, darling. You must tell her he wanted to come.

MARY. I agree. It is the right thing to do.

JANE. I am certain Mr. Grey means only the best by wishing to support Georgiana.

LYDIA. And I think it should be her choice and the rest of us should stay out of it.

> *Everyone is shocked that Lydia wants to stay out of someone's drama.*

What?

KITTY. You're right. All of you. Irritatingly.

LIZZY. I doubt there's a one of us that has not been both irritated and fortified by the rest.

LYDIA. Too true.　**MARY.** Can confirm.　**JANE.** Never irritated.　**KITTY.** HA.

> *The five Bennet sisters are united.*

Scene 4

Outside Georgiana's house, evening, just before the guests arrive.

Henry walks up, holding the gift for Georgiana. He hesitates for a moment, and just as he is about to ring the bell, Georgiana steps outside in a coat, taking a breath of cold air to calm her nerves.

Henry stops, surprised.

GEORGIANA. Mr.…Grey?

HENRY. Miss Darcy.

GEORGIANA. I—Hello—my goodness.

> *Seeing each other freezes them both. There is a pause, a breath, an electricity, a moment between them. Henry recovers and boldly comes forward.*

HENRY. Hello. Please forgive the interruption.

GEORGIANA. You need no forgiveness, Mr. Grey. Just a bit of explanation. It has been so long.

HENRY. It has indeed, and I only wanted to present you with a gift before tonight's concert. In honor of the debut of your Society.

GEORGIANA. You know of the Society? And the concert? Mr. Grey, you appear surprisingly well-informed.

HENRY. Oh. Well. The pamphlets for tonight. I'm working at—well—part owner now of your printing house, you see.

GEORGIANA. You are?

HENRY. I am sorry if my unexpected visit is disturbing right before you are to play.

GEORGIANA. I am not disturbed. It is good to see you, Mr. Grey. Very good.

HENRY. *(Bowing.)* Likewise. After so many years.

GEORGIANA. Too many.

> **HENRY.** Indeed.

GEORGIANA. You live in London?

HENRY. I do.

GEORGIANA. How nice.

HENRY. It is.

Unmistakable sparks fly between them.

GEORGIANA. You will stay for the concert, of course. You must. I recall how fond you are of music. And of course, Mrs. Grey is welcome.

HENRY. Ah, no, there is no Mrs. Grey. Though I suppose my brother's wife would disagree.

GEORGIANA. Then stay. Please.

HENRY. I would so very much love to, but Mrs. O'Brien suggested you were at capacity for the evening.

GEORGIANA. Did she? When?

HENRY. I called. Earlier today. To deliver the pamphlets.

GEORGIANA. I am sorry I missed you. But as for tonight, it is my concert and I say we have room for one more.

HENRY. Only if you are very sure I do not intrude.

GEORGIANA. You do not, Mr. Grey.

HENRY. Then I am honored to celebrate the Society you are creating. You are truly a champion of the cause.

GEORGIANA. Simply a woman with a purpose.

HENRY. To me those are one and the same.

GEORGIANA. I'll be playing a new George Williams concerto. I hope you will enjoy it.

HENRY. I have so often before, I am certain I will again tonight. I am such an admirer…of Williams. I never thought there could be a contemporary of Beethoven who can elicit the depth of artistry and emotion, but with such a profoundly unique voice. Williams does. When *you* play it.

GEORGIANA. You are kind.

HENRY. And if it is not improper, as I said, I have something for you.

Henry gives her a handsomely-bound folio. Georgiana begins to leaf through it.

GEORGIANA. What's this?

HENRY. I have decided to begin publishing music and wanted to start with my favorite. For you, the collected works of…George Williams. It is one of a kind.

GEORGIANA. Mr. Grey, this is an extraordinary gesture.

HENRY. For an extraordinary musician. The first piece is my favorite.

Georgiana turns to the front of the folio. She gasps.

GEORGIANA. Oh. But no, that piece was not composed by George Williams…

HENRY. And yet it belongs in this collection, don't you think?

She looks up at him, feeling completely and totally seen. She smiles.

GEORGIANA. Thank you. So very much.

HENRY. I will leave you and will eagerly await your performance tonight. Miss Darcy.

And he leaves. She takes a steadying breath but her mind is reeling.

She walks back in the house…

Scene 5

Inside her home again, now set up for the salon.

Georgiana enters, walks immediately to Kitty, who is fussing with notes and music at the piano.

KITTY. Georgie, would you prefer to stand to the left or right to make your speech? I have prepared some notes, if you'd like to look them over, and I thought I'd leave the pages just here—

GEORGIANA. Henry Grey was just outside. I spoke to him. He was at my home, for the *second* time today, it would seem.

KITTY. Ah. Yes.

GEORGIANA. You knew.

KITTY. I saw him briefly earlier, but I became overwhelmed with the preparation. I meant to tell you—

GEORGIANA. And yet you did not. How could you fail to mention that he called? And that he is a patron of ours! And that he was in my home!

KITTY. I decided it would be best to not distract you.

GEORGIANA. And you also decided the concert was full and he was not to be invited? How very much you remind me of my brother.

KITTY. Georgie.

GEORGIANA. I have invited him myself, and I humbly request you do not bar him from entry.

KITTY. I did not want to stop him, I just wanted to protect you from being overcome!

GEORGIANA. Do you think I could have accomplished so much in so little time with a world designed to silence me if I were so easily overcome?! The whole point of this Society is so women can decide for themselves. *I will decide for myself. (Deciding.)* I am going to reveal all.

KITTY. What? Wait. No. Please consider all the effort that was put into the announcement of the Society and save the whole of it for a wiser time! This moment is about more than you. This Society is a beacon of hope for so many women and girls. We have worked too hard to risk it all.

GEORGIANA. I am willing to risk all to tell the truth.

KITTY. Well, I am not! Georgiana, please.

GEORGIANA. It is *my* turn to tell *my* truth. You will not decide for me, not my future and not my heart.

> *A heartbreaking moment to find what to say…*

KITTY. Do as you will. The Society is yours.

> *Kitty joins the rest of the family as everyone takes their seats. Henry enters and sits as well.*

MARY. Is that…?

LIZZY. It is! Mr. Grey is here!

LYDIA. So handsome. I told you!

JANE. And such a kind face.

LIZZY. What will Georgiana say?

MARY. Probably something like "hello."

KITTY. She will be fine. It's what she wanted.

DARCY. What is all this about?

LIZZY. Mr. Henry Grey! He has come tonight!

DARCY. Mr. Grey?

THOMAS. Mr. Grey is here?! Tremendous!

LIZZY. Are we sure she will be all right?

DARCY. Why are you so convinced she would care?

LIZZY, JANE, MARY, and LYDIA. *Because she does.*

DARCY. Thomas, do you agree with the women?

THOMAS. I always agree with the women.

> *Georgiana sits at the piano.*
> *The noise of the room quiets.*
> *The concert begins.*

Scene 6

It is just Georgiana, and a piano, Henry and Kitty are just visible in the shadows.

GEORGIANA. Thank you for spending this holiday evening with me, in my home. Tonight we gather to mark the founding of The Society for Women Musicians, the first of its kind in England, created to uplift and encourage women in music—singers, performers, composers.

Many, perhaps even those among you tonight, have doubts. Perhaps you doubt the necessity of a society of this kind, perhaps you doubt the ability or creativity of our members. Perhaps you imagine no woman could compare to Bach, Mozart, Beethoven, or George Williams.

Which is why it is my pleasure to reveal that…
I…
I am George Williams.

> *Gasps.*

I have composed under that name for years knowing that as Georgiana Darcy, my music would have never been heard beyond my drawing room. It is important for you, *(To Henry.)* for all of you, to know that the story I tell is my own.

This, dear friends, is why this Society must be born.
We will be silenced no longer.
We will prove ourselves under our own names.
We demand nothing more than opportunity.
Because we have music within us all. Stories to tell.
All we need is to be heard.

> *She connects with Kitty for a moment.*
>
> *Then she begins to play with such emotion, a song of longing and love.*
>
> *Henry can barely breathe while she plays. He cannot look away.*
> *As Georgiana finishes the song, she looks up, and as the last note lingers she locks eyes with Henry.*
>
> *Blackout.*

Scene 7

> *After the concert, Kitty, Thomas, Mary, Jane, Lydia, Lizzy, and Darcy, gathered around the piano.*

LIZZY. That was wonderful!

THOMAS. I am in tears. Do you see that I am in tears?

DARCY. *(To Lizzy.)* Did you know? Please tell me you did not keep this from me.

LIZZY. I had no idea. I knew Georgiana was an exceptional performer, but this is more than I could have imagined for her!

DARCY. And Mr. Henry Grey was here?! How? Why?

KITTY. Deception.

THOMAS. True love!

DARCY. But how did he come to be invited at all?

KITTY. Deception.

THOMAS. True love!

DARCY. Good lord.

LIZZY. Does it matter?! Our Georgiana is George Williams! She has deceived all of London, all of England!

MARY. And brava to her! Oh, how I do love a woman who outsmarts a nation.

KITTY. She only created opportunity where there was none.

DARCY. Did *you* know?

KITTY. Of course I knew. Who do you think penned all of George Williams' letters? Who has given interviews, arranged publicity, managed resources, negotiated commissions?

THOMAS. You!

KITTY. Yes dear.

MARY. Oh, well done, Kitty!

THOMAS. But how did I not know?

KITTY. Because I am wildly efficient. For years, I have managed a household as well as the persona of a popular, yet reclusive composer. Of course, Georgiana is the true genius of George Williams. I am just his pen.

THOMAS. You are more than anyone's "just." You are the water to the mill; nothing works without you. And keeping a few secrets of your own I might add.

KITTY. Well, no good marriage can survive too much honesty.

JANE. You two are far too alike to stay angry at one another.

THOMAS. Very true.

    Thomas and Kitty kiss. Darcy pulls Lizzy aside.

DARCY. What have I done, Elizabeth?

LIZZY. What do you mean darling? This is a triumph; your sister is a sensation!

DARCY. And yet I, who is meant to love her more than any other, who was meant to *know* her better than any other, found myself the only person in a crowded hall unable to applaud her extraordinary accomplishments? Because I did not see them before now. How have I not seen this wonderful person?

LIZZY. You see her now, and perhaps you and Georgiana can finally become properly acquainted.

> *Georgiana enters. They applaud her.*

LYDIA. Oh, bravo my dear!   **MARY.** Brava!   **THOMAS.** We were just saying how excellent the evening was.

GEORGIANA. Thank you, everyone.

DARCY. Georgiana—

GEORGIANA. *(Pulling Thomas aside.)* Thomas, have you seen Henry?

THOMAS. I believe he went outside.

GEORGIANA. Then I must find him. Excuse me.

DARCY. Please, just a moment of your time—

GEORGIANA. I must go and find Mr. Grey.

DARCY. *You are an extraordinary artist, Georgiana.*

> *This stops Georgiana cold.*

Yes you must go.
I know you must.
Now I know.
Your piece tonight. It was breathtaking, full of love, full of longing. It captured exactly how I feel…about Elizabeth. You somehow were able to convey what I have always kept most private. The love in my heart, in my very soul, for her.
And then I realized that it was, of course, *your* heart on display in that most soaring music and not mine. Because you too have known love. As real as my own.

Your happiness was my responsibility and I failed you. I am so sorry. And I am so proud.

> *This is it, the real apology she has always wanted and the forgiveness he has craved.*

GEORGIANA. Thank you, brother.

> *They embrace. There might be some tears.*

DARCY. And now…?

GEORGIANA. *(Smiling.)* Now I must find Mr. Grey. You need not wait up.

DARCY. Oh, we certainly will.

KITTY. Be serious, Georgie.

THOMAS. Can't sleep tonight.

LIZZY. Of course, we will!

> *Off Georgiana runs.*

Scene 8

> *Outside Georgiana's house.*
>
> *Henry paces, looking up and down the street, anxious.*
>
> *Georgiana walks up, still in her gold evening dress.*

GEORGIANA. Mr. Grey! I could not find you inside. I'd hoped you had not left yet.

HENRY. No. You were rightly surrounded by enthusiasts. And quite frankly, Miss Darcy, I was…overwhelmed.

GEORGIANA. Did you not enjoy it?

HENRY. Oh no, it was…resplendent.

GEORGIANA. Thank you.

HENRY. It is right that the rest of the world now knows your truth. It was, if I may say, the perfect proof. Of your philosophy and of yourself. If Williams is celebrated as a composer, you must be equally celebrated as one. The necessity of your Society is undeniable!

GEORGIANA. Kitty would say that would make an excellent fundraising pamphlet.

>   *Henry smiles.*

The first piece in the volume you gave me…it was the piece that I'd played for you at Pemberley years ago. Which means…you've known this whole time.

HENRY. Since the first Williams concert you played. I was there. I knew no one else but you could have created such wonder. There was no reclusive composer, there was only you. I had not forgotten our conversation around your piano at Pemberley when you said that there was likely no place in this world for your musical voice. But you found one, you earned one, and you did it with the pure gift of your music.

GEORGIANA. How is it, Mr. Grey, even now, you know me so well?

HENRY. I am simply fortunate to know you at all.

>   *Are they going to say everything? Yes. Henry goes for it.*

(A breath.) Miss Darcy, I have many regrets about the events of that Christmas. If I could return to that time, I would trust you with my whole truth, my whole heart. I was ashamed to be from a ruined family, unable to provide all you deserved.

GEORGIANA. You could not possibly regret more than I. That I did not better convey my heart, that I did not fight for you. And that I did not fight for me.

HENRY. You must know, I loved you since I first heard you play. I loved you in every letter I sent. I loved you that one perfect day I was able to say it aloud. I have loved you, for all these years. And I love you still.

GEORGIANA. Still you do?

HENRY. Yes. *(A bit too loud.)* YES. And you? Do you—?

GEORGIANA. *Yes, of course I love you, how many concertos must I write!*

>   *He laughs. She goes to him, takes his hand.*

HENRY. Your hand is shaking.

GEORGIANA. *(Smiles.)* It is Christmas Eve, and I am outside in this ridiculous gown Kitty made me wear. I am frozen.

HENRY. Forgive me!

> *He opens his coat and welcomes her into it. She lays her head on his chest.*

Shall we go inside?

GEORGIANA. In a moment.

> *They are once again without words…but my god are they happy.*

> *Does it begin to snow? Probably should.*

Scene 9

Just before midnight on Christmas Eve in Georgiana's lovely parlor. All except Henry and Georgiana have assembled.

LYDIA. They are just outside, but I cannot hear them at all, can you?

THOMAS. Not a thing.

LYDIA. It's excruciating.

KITTY. Would you leave them to their privacy!

MARY. Why would we do that?! Can you imagine, to see one another again, after all that time?

JANE. And all that heartbreak.

LYDIA. Oh, it's all terribly romantic.

MARY. Most reasonable people prefer to separate the words "terrible" and "romantic."

> *Henry and Georgiana enter, smiling.*

HENRY. Good evening, all.

GEORGIANA. Happy Christmas.

KITTY. Georgie!

MARY. What happened?

LYDIA. Tell us everything!

THOMAS. This is all very suspenseful.

Dramatic pause.

HENRY. Georgiana and I…shall marry in the new year.

Explosion of glee.

LIZZY. Georgiana!   **JANE.** Oh,   **MARY.** Thank   **LYDIA.** At
my word!   goodness.   last!

THOMAS. I'm going to cry again, there's nothing to be done for it.

DARCY. Mr. Grey, please, let me be the first to welcome you to our family. Mrs. Darcy and I could not be happier for you both.

HENRY. Thank you, Mr. Darcy. I do look forward to becoming better acquainted.

DARCY. *(Not easy to say for him.)* As do I, Mr. Grey. And… Please allow me to say how sorry I am. For misjudging you. My deep apologies to you both.

HENRY. Thank you, sir.

GEORGIANA. Thank you, brother. Thank you.

LIZZY. What a night! The concert, the Society, and now this!

DARCY. Well, if there is any way to support you or the Society, I am at the ready.

GEORGIANA. Then you may speak to Kitty, as she is in charge.

KITTY. I am? What? No. The Society is yours.

GEORGIANA. The music is mine, but the Society…it is you. Your spirit and character make possible all we accomplish. You have managed our grand effort from the start, which allows my music— and the music of so many women—to be heard at all. Otherwise our voices would be dismissed as simply an abundance of noise.

KITTY. I love your noise.

GEORGIANA. And I love that you needn't make a sound and still are the most impressive person I have ever known.

THOMAS. She has raised a thousand pounds just tonight!

GEORGIANA. Kitty!

THOMAS. I was so impressed! She got two gentlemen to argue

about who had capacity to contribute more and ended up convincing them both to donate the full amount!

KITTY. Plentiful wine and a bidding war is all you need to fund the arts it seems.

MARY. It's brilliant! And one thousand already, my word!

DARCY. And I shall double it.

LIZZY. Mr. Darcy!

KITTY. Really? Thank you! My god, I am so good at this!

JANE. You truly are.

MARY. Two thousand!

LYDIA. And I shall talk to the earl, patronage is his favorite sport.

KITTY. *(To Georgiana.)* Well, in addition to launching the Society it seems we shall also be planning a wedding.

GEORGIANA. We love each other and after all this time, there is no need for a spectacle. A small wedding in the new year will be perfect.

HENRY. Oh, I certainly agree.

KITTY. WELL, I DON'T.

    LYDIA. Something SMALL?!

        JANE. NoNoNoNoNo.

            LIZZY. A wedding at Pemberley!

                MARY. Weddings are not actually for the bride; they are for her sisters.

DARCY. And brother.

    Georgiana turns to her brother and hugs him.

    The clock chimes midnight—it is officially Christmas Day.

KITTY. Unless your hands are trembling from excitement, Georgiana, I beg of you to play something celebratory.

JANE. Oh, would you?

THOMAS. A Christmas song?

MARY. Something we can sing!

LYDIA. And dance to!

LIZZY. I would love it.

GEORGIANA. It is only fitting.

> *Georgiana plays "Joy to the World" and the gathering sings along.*

ALL.

Joy to the world! The Lord is come;
Let earth receive her King;
Let every heart prepare him room,
And heaven and nature sing,
And heaven and nature sing,
And heaven, and heaven, and nature sing.

> *Georgiana and Henry.*
> *Kitty and Thomas.*
> *Georgiana and Kitty.*
> *Smiles, kisses, SNOW?!*

End of Play

PROPERTY LIST

(Use this space to create props lists for your production)

SOUND EFFECTS

(Use this space to create sound effects lists for your production)

Hello, actors, theatre makers, and theatre fans,

On behalf of Broadway Licensing Global and the author(s) of this work, we thank you for your continued support of the arts and the playwrights you love.

Like every title in our catalogue, this play is covered by copyright law, which ensures authors are rewarded for creating new dramatic work and protects them from theft and abuse of their work. We are compelled to impress upon all who obtain this edition that **this text may not be copied, distributed, or publicly produced in any way,** nor uploaded to any file-sharing websites or software—public or private. Any such action has an immediate and negative effect on the livelihood of the writer(s)—it is also stealing and is against the law. As a result, should you copy, distribute, or publicly produce any part of this text without express written consent and licensed permission from our company—even if no one is being paid and/or admission is not being charged—your organization shall be subject to legal consequences that we are sure you want to avoid.

But we have faith in you and your understanding of these guidelines!

While this acting edition is the only approved text for performance, there may be other editions of the play available for sale. It is important to note that our team has worked with the playwright(s) to ensure this published acting edition reflects their desired text for all future productions. If you have purchased a revised edition from us, that is the only edition you may use for performance, unless explicitly stated in writing by our team.

Finally, and this is an important one, **this script cannot be changed in any way** without written permission from our team. That said, feel free to reach out to us. We don't bite, and we are always happy to have a discussion to see if we can accommodate your request.

We are thrilled this play has made it into your hands and we hope you love it as much as we do. Thank you for helping us keep the theatre alive and well, and for supporting playwrights, in our continued journey to make everyone a theatre person!

Sincerely,
Fellow theatre lovers at Broadway Licensing Global

Note on Songs/Recordings, Images, or Other Production Design Elements

Be advised that Broadway Licensing neither holds the rights to nor grants permission to use any songs, recordings, images, or other design elements mentioned in the play. It is the responsibility of the producing theater/organization to obtain permission of the copyright owner(s) for any such use. Additional royalty fees may apply for the right to use copyrighted materials.

For any songs/recordings, images, or other design elements mentioned in the play, works in the public domain may be substituted. It is the producing theater/organization's responsibility to ensure the substituted work is indeed in the public domain. Broadway Licensing cannot advise as to whether or not a song/arrangement/recording, image, or other design element is in the public domain.

www.ingramcontent.com/pod-product-compliance
Lightning Source LLC
Chambersburg PA
CBHW061039050726
47592CB00004B/1511